John Ashton, S. Baring Gould

The Legendary History of the Cross

A series of sixty-four woodcuts

John Ashton, S. Baring Gould

The Legendary History of the Cross
A series of sixty-four woodcuts

ISBN/EAN: 9783337257125

Printed in Europe, USA, Canada, Australia, Japan

Cover: Foto ©ninafisch / pixelio.de

More available books at **www.hansebooks.com**

The Legendary History of the Cross

A SERIES OF
Sixty-four Woodcuts
From a Dutch book published by
VELDENER, A.D. 1483

WITH

AN INTRODUCTION
Written and Illustrated
By JOHN ASHTON

PREFACE
By S. BARING GOULD, M.A.

London
T. FISHER UNWIN
M.DCCC.LXXXVII

PREFACE.

THE origin of the mediæval romance of the Crofs is hard to difcover. It was very popular. It occurs in a good number of authors, and is depicted in a good many churches in ftained glafs.

I may perhaps be allowed here to repeat what I have faid in my article on the Legend of the Crofs, in " Myths of the Middle Ages : "—

" In the churches of the city of Troyes alone it appears in the windows of four : S. Martin-ès-Vignes, S. Pantaléon, S. Madeleine, and S. Nizier. It is frefcoed along the walls of the choir of S. Croce at Florence, by the hand of Agnolo Gaddi. Pietro della Francefca alfo dedicated his pencil to the hiftory of the Crofs in a feries of frefcoes in the chapel of the Bacci, in the church of S. Francefco at Arezzo. It occurs as a predella painting among the fpecimens of early art at the Accademia delle Belle Arti at Venice, and is the subject of a picture by Beham, in the Munich Gallery. The Legend is told in full in the 'Vita Christi,' printed at Troyes in 1517; in the 'Legenda Aurea' of Jacques de Voragine; in a French MS. of the thirteenth century, in the British Museum. Gervase of Tilbury relates a portion of it in his 'Otia Imperalia,' quoting Peter Comestor; it appears in the 'Speculum Historiale' of Gottfried of Viterbo, in the 'Chronicon Engelhusii,' and elsewhere."

In the very curious Creation window of S. Neot's Church, Cornwall, Seth is represented putting three pips of the Tree of Life into the mouth and nostrils of dead Adam, as he buries him.

Of the popularity of the story of the Cross there can be no doubt, but its origin is involved in obscurity. It is generally possible to track most of the religious and popular folk tales and romances of the Middle Ages to their origin, which is frequently Oriental, but it is not easy to do so with the Legend of the Cross. It would rather seem that it was made up by some romancer out of all kinds of pre-existing material, with no other object than to write a religious novel for pious readers, to displace the sensuous novels which were much in vogue.

We know that this was largely done after the third century, and a number of martyr legends, such as those of S. Apollinaris Syncletica, SS. Cyprian and Justina, the story of Duke Procopius, S. Euphrosyne, SS. Zosimus and Mary, SS. Theophanes and Pansemne, and many others were composed with this object. The earliest of all is undoubtedly the Clementine Recognitions, which dates from a remotely early period, and carries us into the heart of Petrine Christianity, and in which many a covert attack is made on S. Paul and his teaching. On the other hand, we know that an Asiatic priest, as Tertullian tells us, wrote a romance on "Paul and Thecla, out of love to Paul." S. Jerome says that a Pauline zealot, when convicted before his bishop of having written the romance, tried to exculpate himself by saying that he had done it out of admiration for S. Paul, but the Bishop would not accept the excuse, and deprived him. Unfortunately this romance has not come down to us, though we have another on S. Paul and his relations to Thecla, who is said to have accompanied him on his apostolic rambles, disguised in male attire.

The Greek romance literature was not wholesome reading for Christians. Some of the writers of these tales became Christian bishops, and probably devoted their facile pens to more edifying subjects than the difficulties of parted lovers.

Heliodorus, who wrote "Theagenes and Charicheia," is said to have become Bishop of Tricca, in Thessaly. Socrates, in the fifth century, in speaking of clerical celibacy, mentions the severity of the rule imposed on his clergy by this Heliodorus, "under whose name there are love-books extant, called Ethiopica, which he composed in his youth."

Achilles Tatius, author of the "Loves of Clitophon and Leucippe," is said also to have become a bishop. So also Eustathius of Thessalonica, author of the "Lives of Hysemene and Hysmenias," but this is more than doubtful.

Three things conduced to the production of a Christian romance literature in the early ages of the Church :—(1) The necessity under which the Church lay of supplying a want in human nature; (2) The need there was for producing some light wholesome literature to supply the place of the popular love-romances then largely read and circulated ; (3) The fact that some bishops and converts were experienced novel writers, and therefore ready to lend their hands to some better purpose than amusing the leisure and flattering the passions of the idle and young.

Much the same conditions exifted in the Middle Ages. There was an influx of fenfuous literature from the Eaft, through the Arabs of Spain and Sicily; Oriental tales eafily took Weftern garb, in which the caliphs became kings of Chriftendom, and the fakirs and imauns were converted into monks and Catholic priefts. To counteract thefe ftories, collections of which may be found in Le Grand d'Auffi and Von der Hagen, and in Boccaccio, the Gefta Romanorum was drawn up, a collection of moral tales, many of them of fimilar Oriental parentage. But befide thefe fhort ftories, or novels, were long romances, fome heroic, and founded on early national traditions and ballads. To thefe belong the Niebelungen Lied and Noth, the Gudrun, the Heldenbuch, the cycles of Karlovingian and of Arthurian romance.

As it happens, we have two authors in the Middle Ages, living much about the fame time, one intenfely heathen in all his conceptions, the other as entirely Chriftian, each dealing with fubjects from the fame cycle, and the one writing in avowed oppofition to the tendency of the other's book. I allude to Wolfram of Efchenbach and Gottfried of Strafsburg. The latter wrote the Triftram, the former the Parzival. In Gottfried, the moral fenfe feems to be abfolutely dead; there is no perception of the facredneſs of truth, of chaſtity, of honour, none of religion. Wolfram is his exact converſe. Wolfram gives us the hiſtory of the Grail, but he did not invent the myth of the Grail, he derived it from pre-exiſting material. The Grail myth is almoſt certainly heathen in its origin, but it has been entirely Chriſtianiſed. The holy baſin is that in which the Blood of Chriſt is preſerved, and only the pure of heart can ſee it; but the Grail was really the great cauldron of Nature, the baſin of Ceridwen, the earth goddeſs of the Kelts, or, among Teutonic nations, the ſacrificial cauldron of Odin, in which was brewed the ſpirit of poeſy, of the blood of Mimer. The remembrance of the myſterious veſſel remained after Kelt and Teuton had become Chriſtian, and the poets and romanciſts gave it a new ſpell of life by chriſtening it. It was much the ſame with the ſtory of the Croſs. In the Teutonic North, tree worſhip was widely ſpread; the tree was ſacred to Odin, who himſelf, according to the myſterious Havamal, hung nine nights wounded, as a ſacrifice to himſelf, a voluntary ſacrifice, in " the wind-rocked tree."

That tree was Yggdraſill, the world tree, whoſe roots extended to hell, and whoſe branches ſpread to heaven.

Northern mythology is full of allusion to this tree, but we have, unfortunately, little of the history of it preserved to us; we know of it only through allusions. The Christmas tree is its representative; it has been taken up out of paganism, and rooted in Christian soil, where it flourishes to the annual delight of thousands of children.

Now the mediæval romancists laid hold of this tree, as they laid hold of the Grail basin, and used it for Christian purposes. The Grail cup became the chalice of the Blood of Christ, and the Tree of Odin became the Cross of Calvary. They worked into the romance all kinds of material gathered from floating folk-tale of heathen ancestry, and they pieced in with it every scrap of allusion to a tree they could find in Scripture. It is built up of fragments taken from all kinds of old structures, put together with some skill, and built into a goodly romance; but the tracing of every stone to its original quarry has not been done by anyone as yet. The Grail myth has had many students and interpreters, but not the Cross myth. That remains to be examined, and it will doubtless prove a study rewarding the labour of investigation.

S. BARING-GOULD.

The Legendary History of the Cross.

HE Cross on which our Lord and Saviour suffered, would, naturally, if properly authenticated, be an object of the deepest veneration to all Christian men, be their creed, or shade of opinion what it might; but, for over 300 years it could not be found, and it was reserved for the Empress Helena in her old age (for she was 79 years old) to discover its place of concealment.[1] That this *Invention*, or finding of the Cross was believed in, at the time, there can be no manner of doubt, for it is alluded to by

[1] A.D. 326.

St. Cyril, Patriarch of Jerusalem (A.D. 350 to 386), and by St. Ambrose. Rufinus of Aquila, a friend of St. Jerome, in his *Ecclesiastical History,* gives an account of its finding, in the following words: "About the same time, Helena, the mother of Constantine, a woman of incomparable faith, whose sincere piety was equalled by her rare munificence, warned by celestial visions, went to Jerusalem, and inquired of the inhabitants where was the place where the Divine Body had been affixed and hung on a gibbet. This place was difficult to find, for the persecutors of old had raised a statue to Venus,¹ in order that the Christians who might wish to adore Christ in that place, should appear to address their homage to the goddess; and thus it was little frequented, and almost forgotten. After clearing away the profane objects which defiled it, and the rubbish that was there heaped up, she found three crosses placed in confusion. But the joy

Rufinus on the Invention.

Hadrian is said to have done this.

which this discovery caused her was tempered by the impossibility of distinguishing to whom each of them had belonged. There, also, was found the title written by Pilate in Greek, Latin, and Hebrew characters; but still there was nothing to indicate sufficiently clearly the Cross of our Lord. This uncertainty of man was settled by the testimony of heaven." And then follows the story of the dead woman being raised to life.

Not only did Rufinus write thus, but Socrates, Theodoret, and Sozomen, all of whom lived within a century after the *Invention*, tell the same story, so that it must have been of current belief. *Other Authorities.*

The punishment of the Cross was a very ordinary one, and of far wider extent than many are aware. It was common among the Scythians, the Greeks, the Carthaginians, the Germans, and the Romans, who, however, principally applied it to their slaves, and rarely crucified *Punishment of the Cross.*

free men, unless they were robbers or assassins.

Alexander the Great, after taking the city of Tyre, caused two thousand inhabitants to be crucified.

Flavius Josephus relates, in his *Antiquities of the Jews*, that Alexander, the King of the Jews, on the capture of the town of Betoma, ordered eight hundred of the inhabitants to suffer the death of the Cross, and their wives and children to be massacred before their eyes, whilst they were still alive.

Augustus, after the Sicilian War, crucified six thousand slaves who had not been claimed by their masters.

Tiberius crucified the priests of Isis, and destroyed their temple.

Titus, during the siege of Jerusalem, crucified all those unfortunates who, to the number of five or six hundred daily, fled from the city to escape the famine; and so numerous were these executions, that crosses were wanting,

History of the Cross.

and the land all about seemed like a hideous forest.

These instances are sufficient to show that death by crucifixion was a common punishment; but, singularly enough, the shape of the Cross has never been satisfactorily settled; practically, the question lies between the *Crux capitata*, or *immissa*, which is the ordinary form of the Latin Cross, and the *Crux ansata*, or *commissa*, frequently called the *Tau* Cross, from the Greek letter **T**. The *Tau*-shaped Cross is, undoubtedly, to be met with most frequently in the older representations; and the more ancient authorities, such as Tertullian, St. Jerome, St. Paulinus, Sozomen, and Rufinus, are of opinion that this was the shape of the Cross. After the fifteenth century, our Lord is rarely depicted on the *Crux commissa*, it being reserved for the two thieves.

M. Adolphe Napoleon Didron, in his *Iconographie Chretienne*, gives a few illustrations of the antiquity of the

The different sorts of Crosses.

Antiquity of the Tau Cross.

Tau Cross: "The Cross is our crucified Lord in person; 'Where the Cross is, there is the martyr,' says St. Paulinus. Consequently it works miracles, as does Jesus Himself: and the list of wonders operated by its power is in truth immense. By the simple sign of the Cross traced upon the forehead or the breast, men have been delivered from the most imminent danger. It has constantly put demons to flight, protected the virginity of women, and the faith of believers; it has restored men to life, or health, inspired them with hope or resignation.

"Such is the virtue of the Cross, that a mere allusion to that sacred sign, made even in the Old Testament, and long before the existence of the Cross, saved the youthful Isaac from death, redeemed from destruction an entire people whose houses were marked by that symbol, healed the envenomed bites of those who looked at the serpent raised in the form of a *Tau* upon a pole. It called back the foul into the dead body of the fon of that poor widow who had given bread to the prophet.

"A beautiful painted window, belonging to the thirteenth century, in the Cathedral of Bourges, has a reprefentation of Ifaac bearing on his fhoulders the wood that was to be ufed in his facrifice, arranged in the form of a Crofs; the Hebrews, too, marked the lintel of their dwellings with the blood of the Pafchal lamb, in the form of a *Tau* or Crofs without a fummit. The widow of Sarepta picked up and held crofswife two pieces of wood, with which fhe intended to bake her bread. Thefe figures, to which others alfo may be added, ferve to exalt the triumph of the Crofs, and feem to flow from a grand central picture which forms their fource, and exhibits Jefus expiring on the Crofs. It is from that real Crofs indeed, bearing the Saviour, that thefe fubjects from the Old Teftament derive all their virtue."

The Tau Crofs.

Wood of the Cross.

The wood of which it was made is as unsettled as its shape. The Venerable Bede says that our Lord's Cross was made of four kinds of wood: the inscription of box, the upright beam of cypress, the transverse of cedar, and the lower part of pine. John Cantacuméne avers that only three woods were employed: the upright, cedar; the transverse, pine; and the head in cypress. Others say that the upright was cypress, the transverse in palm, and the head in olive; or cedar, cypress, and olive. Most authorities seem to concur that it was made of several woods, but there is a legend that it was made from the aspen tree, whose leaves still tremble at the awful use the tree was put to; whilst that veritable traveller, Sir John Maundeville, says: "And also in Iherusalem toward the Weast is a fayre church where the tree grew of the which the Crosse was made." Lipsius says that it was made of but one wood, and that was oak; but M. Rohault de Fleury (to whose wonderful and comprehensive work, *Mémoire sur les Instruments de la Passion de notre Sauveur Jesus Christ*, I am deeply indebted, says, "M. Decaisne, member of the Institut, and M. Pietro Savi, professor at the University of Pisa, have shewn me by the microscope that the pieces in the Church of the Holy Cross of Jerusalem at Rome, in the Cathedral at Pisa, in the Duomo at Florence, and in Notre Dame at Paris, were of *pine*." And he adds, in a footnote, "Independently of the experiments which M. Savi kindly made in my presence, he wrote me the results of other observations, which tended to confirm."

Starting with the Invention of the Holy Cross, the loving, but fervid, imaginations of the faithful soon wove round it a covering of imagery, as we have just seen in the case of the several woods of the Cross, and the sacred tree became the subject of a legend (for so it always was only meant to be), which

Cross made of pine.

The Legendary

Caxton's Golden Legend

was incorporated in the *Legenda Aurea Sanctorum*, or *Golden Legend of the Saints*, of Jacobus de Voragine, a collection of legends connected with the services of the Church. This book was exceedingly popular, and, when Caxton set up his printing-press at Westminster, he produced a translation, the history of which he quaintly tells us in a preface.*

As this Golden Legend is the standard authority on the subject, and as it will

---

* "And for as moche as this fayd worke was grete & over chargeable to me taccomplisshe, I feryd me in the begynnynge of the translacion to have contynued it / bycause of the longe tyme of the translacion / & also in thenpryntyng of ye same and in maner halfe desperate to have accomplissd it / was in purpose to have lefte it / after that I had begonne to translate it / & to have layed it aparte ne had it be(en) at thynstance & requeste of the puyssant noble & vertuous erle my lord wyllyam erle of arondel / whych desyred me to procede & contynue the said werke / & promysed me to take a resonable quantyte of them when they were acheyeued & accomplisshed / and sente to me a worshypful gentylman a servaunt of his named John Stanney which solycyted me in my Lordes name that I shold in no wyse leve it but accomplisshe it promysyng that my sayd lord shold duringe my lyf geve & graunt to me a yerely fee / that is to wete a bucke in sommer / & a doo in Wynter / with whiche fee I holde me wel contente," &c.

History of the Cross.

much assist the intelligent appreciation of the wood-blocks, I reproduce it, premising that I have used throughout the first edition, 20 Nov., 1483:—

'But alle the dayes of adam lyvynge here in erthe amounte to the somme of ix Cccc* yere / And in thende of his lyf

[1] Page 39.

Length of Adam's life.

* This apparently long life of Adam is admitted on all hands, even in the Revised Version of the Bible. The Talmud says that God promised him one thousand years of life, and it is recorded that he begat Seth when he was a hundred and thirty years old. On this the Talmud (*Eruvin*, fol. 18, col. 2) has the following comment: "Rav Yirmyah ben Elazer said: All those years, which Adam spent in alienation from God, he begat evil spirits, demons, and fairies; for it is said, 'And Adam was an hundred and thirty years, and begat a son in his own likeness, after his image'; consequently, before that time, he begat after another image."

This term of one hundred and thirty years seems to have been a period in Adam's existence, for we again find (*Eruvin*, fol. 18 b.): "Adam was a Chasid, or great saint, when he observed that the decree of death was occasioned by him; he *fasted* a hundred and thirty years, and all this time he abstained from intercourse with his wife."

There is a Talmudical tradition that God showed the future to Adam (Avoth d'Rab. Nathan, chap. 31): "The Holy One—blessed be He!—shewed unto Adam each generation, and its preachers, its guardians, its leaders, its prophets, its heroes, its sinners, and its saints, saying, 'In such and such a generation such and such a *King* shall reign, in such and such a generation such and such a wise man shall teach.'"

Talmud legends respecting Adam's length of life.

xx

Of thynuencyon of tholy
crosse / and first of thys worde
Inuencion.

History of the Cross.

whan he fhold dye / it is faid but ot none auctoryte / that he fente Seth his fone in to paradys for to fetch the oyle of mercy / where he receyuyde certayn graynes of the fruyt of the tree of mercy by an angel / And whan he come agayn / he fonde his fader adam yet alyve and told hym what he had don. And thenne

---

This is amplified in Midrafh Yalkut (fol. 12), where it is faid that God fhowed Adam all future generations of men, with their leaders, learned and literary men, and there he obferved that David was credited with only three hours of life, and he faid, "Lord and Creator of the world, is this unalterable?" "Such was my firft intention," was the reply. "How many years have I to live?" afked Adam. "One thoufand." Then Adam faid, "I will lend him fome of my years." And a document was drawn up whereby Adam transferred feventy years of his life to David.

S. Baring-Gould, in his legends of *Old Teftament Characters*, vol i. p. 77, referring to a Muffulman legend, fays: "Finally, when Adam reached his nine hundred and thirtieth year, the Angel of Death appeared under the form of a goat, and ran between his legs.

"Adam recoiled with horror, and exclaimed, 'God has given me one thoufand years; wherefore comeft thou now?'

"'What!' exclaimed the Angel of Death, 'haft thou not given feventy years of thy life to the prophet David?'

"Adam ftoutly denied that he had done fo. Then the Angel of Death drew the document of transfer from out of his beard, and prefented it to Adam, who could no longer refufe to go."

xxii	The Legendary
Laughed or smiled.¹	Adam lawhed¹ firſt / and then deyed / and thenne he leyed the greynes or kernellis under his faders tonge and buryed hym / in the vale of ebron / and out of his mouth grewe thre trees of the thre graynes / of which the croſſe that our lord ſuffred his paſſion on / was made by vertue of which he gate² very mercy and was brought out of darknes in to veray light of heven / to the whiche he brynge us that lyveth and regneth god world with oute ende.
² *Obtained true mercy.*	
³ *Page 167.* *Of old.*	THE ³Invencion* of the holy croſſe is ſaid bycauſe that this day the holy croſſe was founden / for to fore⁴ it was founden of ſeth in paradyſe tereſtre / lyke as hit ſhal be ſayd here after / and alſo it was founden of ſalamon in the mounte of lybane and of the quene of ſaba / in the temple of ſalamon / And of the

* The Feſtival of the Invention, or finding of the Croſs, is kept in the Roman and Engliſh Churches on May 3.

Iewes in the water of pyscyne* / And on thys day it was founden of Helayne in the mounte of Calvarye/.

Of the Holy Crosse.

THE holy crosse was founden two hondred yere after the resurrexyon of our lord / It is redde in the gospel of nychodemus† / that whan adam wexyd seck / Seth hys sone wente to the gate of paradyse terestre, for to gete the oyle of

---

* Piscina, a fish-pond: *Lat.* In this instance it is supposed to be the Pool of Bethesda.

† Nicodemus, chap. 14:—

But when the first man our father Adam heard these things, that Jesus was baptized in Jordan, he called out to his son Seth, and said, *v.* 1.

Declare to your sons, the patriarchs and prophets, all those things which thou didst hear from Michael the Archangel, when I sent thee to the gates of Paradise to entreat God that he would anoint my head when I was sick. *v.* 2.

Then Seth, coming near to the patriarchs and prophets, said: I, Seth, when I was praying to God at the gates of Paradise, beheld the angel of the Lord, Michael, appear unto me, saying, I am sent unto thee from the Lord; I am appointed to preside over human bodies. *v.* 3.

I tell thee, Seth, do not pray to God in tears, and entreat him for the oil of the tree of mercy, wherewith to anoint thy father Adam for his headach; *v.* 4.

mercy for to enoynte wythal hys faders body / Thenne apperyd to hym faynt mychel thaungel and fayd to hym / travayle not the in vayne / for thys oyle / for thou mayft not have it till fyve thoufand and fyve hondred yere been paffed / how be it that fro Adam unto the paffyon of our lord were but fyve ⅿⅽ and 𝔵𝔵𝔵𝔦𝔦𝔦 yere / In another place it is redde that the aungel broughte hym a braunche / and commaunded hym to plante it in the mounte of lybanye / Yet

v. 5. Becaufe thou canft not by any means obtain it till the laft day and times, namely, till five thoufand and five hundred years be paft.

v. 6. Then will Chrift, the moft merciful Son of God, come on earth to raife again the human body of Adam, and at the fame time to raife the bodies of the dead, and when he cometh he will be baptized in Jordan;

v. 7. Then with the oil of his mercy he will anoint all thofe that believe on him; and the oil of his mercy will continue to future generations, for thofe who fhall be born of the water and the Holy Ghoft unto eternal life.

v. 8. And when at that time the moft merciful Son of God, Chrift Jefus, fhall come down on earth, he will introduce our father Adam into Paradife, to the tree of mercy.

v. 9. When all the patriarchs and prophets heard all thefe things from Seth, they rejoiced more.

fynde we in another place / that he gafe
to hym of the tree that Adam ete of /
And fayd to hym that whan that bare
fruyte he fhould be guariffhed[1] and alle
hoole[2] /. whan feth came ageyn he founde
his fader deed / and planted this tree
upon his grave / And it endured there
un to the tyme of Salomon / and bycaufe
he fawe that it was fayre, he dyd[3] doo
hewe it doun / and fette it in his hows
named faltus / and whan the quene of
faba came to vyfyte Salamon / She worfhypped this tre bycaufe fhe fayd the
favyour of alle the world fhold be hanged
there on / by whome the royame[4] of the
Iewes that be defaced and feace.[5] Salomon
for this caufe made hit to be taken up /
& dolven[6] depe in the grounde. Now it
happed after that they of Ierufalem (dyd
do make a grete pytte for a pyfcyne[7] /
where at the mynyfters of the temple
fholde weffhe theyre beftys / that they
fhold facrefyfe / and there founde thys
tre / and thys pyfcyne had fuche vertue,

[1] *Cured:* French, *guerir,* to heal.
[2] *Whole.*
[3] *Did fo—caufed to be:* words of frequent occurrence.
[4] *Kingdom:* French, *royaume.*
[5] *Ceafe.*
[6] *Dug, p. part. of delve.*
[7] *Pond.*

that the aungels defcended and mevyd the water / and the firft feke man that defcendyd in to the water after the mevyng / was made hole of what fomever fekeneffe he was feek of. And whan the tyme approched of the paffyon of our lord / thys tree aroos out of the water and floted above the water / And of this pyece of tymbre made the Iewes the croffe of our lord / Thenne after this hyftorye / the croffe by which we been faved / came of the tree by whiche we were dampned. And the water of that pyfcyne had not his vertue onely of the aungel / but of the tre /. With this tre wherof the croffe was maad / there was a tree that went over thwarte / on whiche the armes of our lord were nayled /. And another pyece above which was the table / wherin the tytle was wryten / and another pyece wherein the fokette or mortys was maad that the body of the croffe ftood in foo that there were foure manere of trees / That

History of the Cross.

is of palme of cypres / of cedre and of olyve. So eche of thyse foure pyeces was of one of those trees /. This blessed crosse was put in the erthe and hyd by the space of on hondred yere and more / But the moder of themperour which was named helayne* founde it in thys manere / For Constantyn came wyth a grete multytude of barbaryns nygh unto the ryver of the dunoe / whyche wold have goon over for to have destroyed alle the contree / And whan constantyn had

---

* Alban Butler, in *The Lives of the Fathers, Martyrs, aud other Principal Saints*, denies that St. Helena was an Innholder (*Stabularia*) in Bithynia, when Constantius married her, and says: "We are assured by the unanimous tradition of our English historians that this holy empress was a native of our island. William of Malmesbury, the principal historian of the ancient state of our country after Bede, and before him, the Saxon author of the life of St. Helen, in 970, quoted by Usher, expressly say that Constantine was a Briton by birth." Leland, in his *Commentarii de Scriptoribus Britannicis*, says that St. Helena was the only daughter of King Coilus, the King Cöol who first built walls round Colchester, and the English Church has generally recognised her British origin. Her festival is kept on August 18.

When her husband, Constantine Chlorus, entered into an arrangement with Diocletian, by which he had the countries

assembled his hooft / He went and sette them ageynst that other partye / But as sone as he began to passe the ryver / he was moche aferde / by caufe he shold on the morne have batayle / and in the nyght as he slepte in his bedde / an aungel awoke hym / and shewed to hym the sygne of the crosse in heven / and sayd to hym / Beholde on hye on heven /. Thanne sawe he the crosse made of ryght clere lyght / & was wryten there upon wyth lettres of golde / In this sygne thou shalte over come the batayle /

---

this side the Alps, namely, Gaul and Britain, he was obliged, as part of the bargain, to divorce St. Helena, and marry Theodora, the daughter-in-law of Maximinianus. According to Eusebius, she was not converted to Christianity at the same time as her son Constantine, who, when he came to the throne, paid her the greatest deference, and gave her the title of Augusta, or empress. After the Council of Nice, in 325, he wrote to Macarius, Bishop of Jerusalem, concerning the building of a splendid church upon Mount Calvary, and St. Helena, although she was then 79 years of age, undertook to see it carried out.

It was then that the reputed Invention of the Cross, together with the nails, took place, and she soon afterwards died, but the exact year is uncertain, some authorities giving A.D. 326, others 328.

Thenne was he alle comforted of thys vyſion / And on the morne / he put in his banere the Croſſe[1] / and made it

[1] The Labārum, or Sacred Banner of Conſtantine.

to be borne tofore hym and his hooſt / And after ſmote in the hooſt of his enemyes / and ſlewe and chaced grete plente / After thys he dyd doo[2] calle the byſſhoppes of the ydolles / and demaunded them to what god the ſygne of the croſſe apperteyned. And whan they coude not anſwere / ſome criſten men that were there tolde to hym the myſterye of the croſſe / and enformed hym in the faythe of the trynyte / Thenne anone he bylevyd parfytly (in) god / and dyd do baptyſe hym / and after, it happed that conſtantyn his ſone remembred the vyctorye of his fader / Sente to helayn his modre

[2] Cauſed to be called together.

for to fynde the holy croſſe / Thenne
helayne wente in to Iheruſalem / and
dyd doo aſſemble all the wyſe men of
the contre / and whan they were aſſem-
bled / they wold fayn knowe wherfore
they were called / Thenne one Iudas
ſayd to them / I wote[1] wel that ſhe wyl
knowe of us where the croſſe of Iheſu
criſte was leyed / but beware you al
that none of you tell hyr / for I wote
wel then ſhall our lawe be deſtroyed /
For zacheus my olde[2] fader ſayde to
ſymon my fader / And my fader ſayde
to me at his dethe / be wel ware / that
for no tormente that ye may ſuffre / telle
not where the croſſe of Iheſu criſte was
leyde / for after that hit ſhal be founden
/ the Iewes ſhal reygne no mour / But
the criſten men that worſhypped the
croſſe ſhal then reygne / And verayly
this Iheſus was the ſone of god.

Then demaunded I my fader / wherfore had they hanged hym on the croſſe
ſythe it was knowen that he was the ſone

[1] Know.

[2] Grandfather.

of god / thenne he fayd to me fayre fone I never accorded thereto / But gayn faid it alwaye / But the Pharifees dyd it bycaufe he repreyvd theyr vyces / but he aroos on the thyrd day / and his dyfciples feeing / he afcended in to heven / Thenne by caufe that Stephen thy broder belevyd in him / the Iewes ftoned hym to dethe.

Then when Iudas had fayd theyfe wordes to his felawes / they anfwerd we never herde of fuche thynges / never the leffe kepe the wel if the quene demaunde the therof / that thou fay no thynge to hyr / Whan the quene had called them / and demaunded them the place where our lord Ihefu crifte had been crucefyed / they wold never tell her nor enfygne[1] her /. Then commaunded fhe to brenne[2] them alle /. But then they doubted and were aferde / & delyvered Iudas to hyr and fayd / lady thys man is the fone of a prophete and of a jufte man / and knoweth right wel the lawe / & can

[1] Inform.
[2] Burn.

telle to you al thynge that ye ſhal demaunde hym /.

Thenne the quene lete al the other goo, and reteyned Iudas without moo[1] /. Thenne ſhe ſhewed to hym his life & dethe & bade hym cheſe whyche he wold. Shewe to me ſayd ſhe the place named golgota where our lord was crucefyed / by cauſe and to the end that we may fynde the croſſe /. Thenne ſayd Iudas, it is two hondred yere paſſed & more / & I was not thenne yet borne. Thenne ſayd to hym the lady / by him that was crucyfyed / I ſhal make the periſſe for hungre / yf thou telle not to me the trouthe.

Thenne made ſhe hym to be caſte into a drye pytte / and there tormented hym by hungre / and evyl reſte / whan he had been ſeuen dayes in that pytte / thenne ſayd he yf I myght be drawen out / he ſhold ſay the trouthe / Thenne he was drawen out / and whan he came to the place / anone the erthe moevyd

[1] *More ado.*

History of the Cross.

and a fume of grete fwettneffe was felte in fuche wyfe that Iudas fmote his hondes togyder for ioye / and fayd / in trouthe Ihefu crifte thou art the favyour of the worlde.

It was fo that adryan the Emperour had doo make in the fame place where the croffe laye a temple of a goddeffe by caufe that all they that come in that place fhold adoure that goddeffe /. But the quene did doo deftroy the temple / Thenne Iudas made hym redy and began to dygge / and whan he came to xx paas[1] depe / he fonde three croffes and broughte them to the quene / And bycaufe he knewe not whiche was the croffe of our lord / he leyed them in the myddel of the cyte / and abode the demonftraunce of god / and aboute the houre of none / there was the corps of a yonge man brought to be buryed / Iudas reteyned the byere / and layed upon hit one of the croffes / and after the fecond / and whan he leyed on hit

[1] *Twenty Paces.*

the third / anone the body that was dede came ageyn to lyf /.

Thenne cryed the devyll in the eyre Iudas what haſt thou doon / thou haſt doon the contrarye that thother Iudas dyd /. For by hym I have wonne many ſowles / and by the I ſhal loſe many / by hym I reygned on the peple / And by the I have loſt my royame / never the leſſe I ſhal yelde to the this bountee /. For I ſhal ſend one that ſhal punyſſhe the / and that was accomplyſſhed by Iulian the apoſtata / which tormented hym afterward whan he was byſſhop of Iheruſalem / and whan Iudas herde hym he curſed the devyl and ſayd to hym / Iheſu cryſte dampne the in fyre pardurable¹ /. After this Iudas was baptyzed and was named quyryache * /. And after was made byſſhop of Iheruſalem /. Whan helayn had the croſſe of Iheſu criſte / and ſaw ſhe had not the nayles / Thenne he dyd

¹ Everlaſting.

---

* Other accounts ſay the Croſſes were found by Macarius, then Biſhop of Jeruſalem.

History of the Cross.

dygge in therthe fo longe / that he founde them fhynyng as golde /. thenne bare he them to the quene / and anone as fhe fawe them fhe worfhypped them wyth grete reverence /.

Thenne gafe faynt helayn a part of the croffe to hir fone / And that other parte fhe lefte in Iherufalem clofyd in golde / fylver and precious ftones /.

And hyr fone bare the nayles to themperour / And the emperour dyd do fette them in hys brydel and in hys helme whan he wente to batayle /. This referreth Eufebe whiche was byffhop of Cezayr[1] / how be it that other fay otherwyfe /. Now it happed that Iulyan the appoftate dyd doo[2] flee quyriache that was byffhop of Iherufalem / by caufe he had founde the croffe / for he hated hit foo mooche / that where fomever he founde the croffe / he dyd hit to be deftroyed / For whan he wente in batayle ageynfte them of perfe / he fente and commaunded quyriache to make facrefyfe

[1] *Eufebius, Bifhop of Cefaræa.*
[2] *Killed.*

to thydolles / and whan he wold not doo hit / he dyd do fmyte of his right honde / and fayd wyth this honde haft thou wryten many letters / by whyche thou repellyd moche folke fro doynge facrefyfe to our goddes /.

Quyriache fayd thou wood hounde[1] thou hift doon to me grete prouffyte / For thou haft cut of the hande / wyth whiche I have many tymes wreton to the fynagoges that they fhold not byleve in Ihefu crifte / and now fythe[2] I am criften / thou haft taken from me that whiche noyed me / thenne dyd Iulyan do melte leed, and cafte it in his mowthe / and after dyd doo brynge a bedde of yron / and made quyriache to be layed and ftratched theron / and after leyed under brennyng cooles / and threwe therein grece and falte / for to torment hym the more / and whan quyriache moved not / Iulyan themperour faid to hym / outher thou fhalt facrefyfe (to) our goddes / or thou fhalt fay at the

---

[1] Mad dog.

[2] Since.

History of the Cross.

leste thou art not cristen/. And whan he sawe he wolde not do never neyther / he dyd doo make a depe pytte ful of serpentes and venemous bestys / and caste hym therein / & whan he entred / anone the serpentes were al deed/. Thenne Iulyan put hym in a cawdron ful of boylyng oyle / and whan he shold entre in to hit / he blessyd it & sayd / Fayre lord torne thys bane to baptysm of marterdom / Thenne was Iulyan moche angry / and commaunded that he should be ryven thorough his herte with a swerde / and in this manere he fynysshed his lyff.

The vertue of the crosse is declared to us by many miracles / For it happed on a tyme that one enchantour had dysceyved a notarye / and brought hym to a place / where he had assembled a grete companye of devylles / and promysed to hym to have muche rychesse / and whan he came there / he saw one persone blacke syttynge on a grete chayer / And

Turn this evil

all aboute hym al ful of horyble people and blacke whiche had speres and swerdes / Thenne demaunded thys grete devyll of the enchantour / who was that clerke / thenchantour sayd to hym / Syr he is oures / thenne sayd the devyl to hym yf thou wylte worshyp me and be my servaunte / and denye Ihesu cryste / thou shalt sytte on my right syde / The clerke anone blessyd hym wyth the sygne of the crosse / and sayd that he was the servaunte of Ihesu criste / his savyour / And anone as he had made the crosse / that grete multitude of devylles vanysshed aweye. It happed that this notarye after this on a tyme entryd with hys lord in the chyrche of saynt sophye / & knelyd doun on his knees to fore the ymage of the crucyfyxe / the which crucifyxe as it semed loked moche openly and sharpelye on hym /. Thenne his lord made hym to go aparte on another syde / and alleweye the crucifixe torned his eyen toward hym /. Thenne he made hym goo on the lefte fyde / and yet the crucifixe loked on hym / Thenne was the lord moche admerveyled / and charged hym & commaunded hym that he fhold telle hym wherof he had fo deferved that the crucifyxe fo behelde and loked on hym / Thenne fayde the notarye that he coude not remembre hym of no good thynge that he had doon / faufe that one tyme he wold not renye nor forfake the crucifixe tofore the devyl /.

Thenne late us fo bleffe us with the fygne of the bleffyd croffe that we may therby be kepte fro the power of our ghooftly and dedely enemye the devyl / and by the glorious paffyon that our faveour Ihefu cryft fuffred on the croffe after this lyf we may come to his everlaftyng blyffe amen /.

Thus endeth thynvencion of the holy croffe.

xl

Here foloweth the Exaltacion of the holy Crosse

Exaltation of the holy Croſſe[1] is ſayd / bycauſe that on this daye the hooly croſſe & faythe were gretely enhaunced /. And it is to be underſtonden that tofore the paſſion of our lord Iheſu cryſte / the tree of the croſſe was a tree of fylthe / For the croſſes were made of vyle trees, & of trees without fruyte / For al that was planted on the Mount of Calvarye bare no fruyt. It was a fowle place / for hit was the place of torment of thevys / It was derke / for it was in a derke place and without any beaute / It was the tree of deth / for men were put there to dethe / It was alſo the tree of ſtenche / for it was planted amonge the caroynes[2] / & after the paſſyon the Croſſe was moche enhaunced / For the Vylte[3] was tranſ-ported into precyouſyte / Of the whiche the bleſſyd ſaynt Andrewe ſayth / O precious holy Croſſe god ſave the / his bareynes was torned into fruyte / as it is ſayd in the Cantyques / I ſhall aſcende up in to a palme tree / et cetera / His

[1] *The Roman and Engliſh Churches celebrate this Feſtival on February 14.*

[2] *Carrion.*

[3] *Vileneſs.*

ignobylyte or unworthynes was tourned into sublymyte and heyght / The Crosse that was tormente of thevys is now born in the front of themperours / his derkenes is torned into lyght and clerenesse / wherof Chrysostom sayth the Crosse and the Woundes shall be more shynyng than the rayes of the Sonne at the jugement / his deth is converted into perdurabylyte of lyf / whereof it is sayd in the preface / that fro hens the lyf resourded¹ / and the stenche is torned into swetenes / canticorum /. This exaltacion of the hooly crosse is solempnysed and halowed solempnly of the Chirche / For the faythe is in hit moche enhaunced /.

For the yere of oure lord five honderd & ƴƀ / our lord suffred his people moche to be tormentyd by the cruelte of the paynyms / And Cosdroe² Kynge of the Perceens subdued to his empyre all the Royaumes of the world / And he cam into Iherusalem and was aferd and a dred of the sepulcre of our lord &

---

¹ Resourced or replenished.

² Chosroes II., who reigned in the seventh Century.

retorned / but he bare with hym the parte of the hooly Croſſe / that ſaynte Helene had left ther. And then he wold be worſhiped of alle the peple / as a god / & dyd do make a tour of gold and of ſylver wherein precious ſtones ſhone / and made therein the ymages of the ſonne and of the mone and of the ſterres / and made that by ſubtyle conduytes water to be hydde / and to come doune in the maner of rayne / And in the laſte ſtage he made horſes to draw charyotes round aboute lyke as they had mevyd the toure / and made it to ſeme as it had thondred / and delyvered his Royaume to his ſone. And thus this curſyd man abode in this Temple / and dyd doo ſette the croſſe of our lord by hym and commaunded that he ſhold be callyd god of alle the peple / And as it is redde in libro de mitrali* officio the ſaid Coſdroe reſydent in his trone as a fader /

---

* The book of the office of Mithras or Mithra, the Sun, worſhipped by the Perſians.

The Legendary

fette the tree of the Croffe on his ryght fyde in ftede of the fonne / and a cock in the lyft fyde in ftede of the hooly ghooft / & commaunded / that he fhold be called fader /. And then Heracle* themperour affembled a grete hooft / and cam for to fyght wyth the fonne of Cofdroe by the ryver of danubie / & thenne hit pleafyd to eyther prynce / that eche of them fhold fyght one ageynfte that other upon the brydge / & he that fhold vaynquyffhe & overcome his adverfarye fholde be prynce of thempyre withoute hurtyng eyther of bothe hostes / & fo hit was ordeyned & fworn / & that who fomever fhold helpe his prynce fhold have forthwith his legges & armes cut of / & to be plonged / & caft in to the Ryver.

And then Heracle commaunded hym all to god and to the hooly croffe wyth all the devocion that he myght. And

---
* Heraclius, Emperor of the Eaft, who from A.D. 622 to 627 fought Chofroes II., defeated him, and concluded peace.

thenne they fought longe / And at the laſt our lord gaf the vyctory to Heracle and ſubdued hym to his empyre / The hooſt that was contrary / and alle the peple of Coſdroe obeyed them to the Cryſten faythe / and receyved the hooly baptyſme / And Coſdroe knew not the end of the batayll / For he was adoured and worſhiped of alle the peple as a god / ſo that no man durſt ſay nay to him / And thenne Heracle came to hym / and fonde hym ſyttinge in his ſyege[1] of golde / and ſayd to hym / For as moche as after the manere thou haſt honoured the Tree of the Croſſe / yf thou wyld receyve baptym and the faythe of Iheſu Cryſt / I ſhal gete it to the / and yet ſhalt thow holde thy crowne and Royamme with lytel hoſtages / And I ſhall lete the have thy lyf / and yf thou wylt not / I ſhall ſlee the wyth my ſwerde / and ſhalle ſmyte of thyne heed / and whanne he wold not accorde therto / he did anon do ſmyte of his hede / and commaunded

Throne, or ſeat; French, ſiège.

that he fhold be buryed / by caufe he had be(en) a Kynge /. And he fonde with hym one his fone of the age of ten yere / whome he dyd doo baptyfe and lyft hym fro the fonte / and left to hym the Royaume of his fader / and then he dyd doo breke that Toure / And gaf the fylver to them of his hoofte / and gaf the gold and precious ftones for to repayre the chirches that the tyraunt had deftroyed / and tooke the hoole croffe / and brought it ageyne to Ierufalem / and as he defcended from the mount of Olyvete / and wold have entryd by the gate by whiche our favyour wente to his paffyon on horfbacke adourned as a Kynge / fodenly the ftones of the gates defcended / and ioyned them togyder in the gate like a wall & all the peple was abafhed[1] / and thenne the Aungel of oure lord appyeryd upon the gate holdyng the figne of the figne (*sic*) of the Croffe in his honde / and fayd / Whanne the Kynge of heven went to his paffion

---

[1] *Aftonifhed.*

by this gate / he was not arayed like a
Kynge / ne on horsbake / but cam
humbly upon an asse / in shewynge
thexample of humylite which he left to
them that honoure hym. And when
this was sayd / he departed and vanysshed
aweye / Thenne th'emperour took of his
hosen and shone[1] himself in wepynge /
and despollyed hymselfe of alle his clothes
in to his sherte / and tooke the crosse of
oure lord / and bare it moche humbly
into the gate / and anone the hardnes of
the stones felte the celestyalle commaundement / and remeved anone / and opened
and gaf entree unto them that entred /
Thenne the sweete odour that was felt
that day whanne the hooly Crosse was
taken fro the Toure of Cosdroe / and
was brought ageyne to Iherusalem fro so
ferre countre / and so grete space of
londe retourned in to Iherusalem in that
moment / and replenysshed it with al
swetnes / Thenne the ryght devoute
Kyng beganne to saye the praysynges of

[1] Shoen—shoes.

the Crosse in this wyse / O Crux splendydior / et cetera / O Crosse more shynynge than alle the Sterres / honoured of the world / right holy / and moche amyable to alle men / whiche only were worthy to bere the raunson of the world Swete tree / Swete nayles / Swete yron / Swete spere berynge the swete burthens / Save thou this present company / that is this daye assembled in thy lawe and praysynges /. And thus was the precious tree of the Crosse re establysshed in his place / and the auncient myracles renewed /. For a dede man was reysed to lyf / and foure men taken with the palsey were cured and heled / ȝ lepres were made clene / and fyften blynde receyved theyr syghte ageyn / Devylles were put out of men / and moche peple / and many / were delyvered of dyverse sekenes and maladyes /. Thenne themperour dyd doo repayre the Chirches / and gaf to them grete geftes / And after retorned home to his Empyre / And hit is said in the Cronycles that this was done otherwise / For they say that whanne Cosdroe hadde taken many Royammes / he took Iherusalem / and Zacharye the patriarke / and bare aweye the tree of the Crosse / And as Heracle wold make pees with hym / the Kyng Cosdroe swore a grete othe / that he wold never make pees with Crysten men and Romayns / yf they denyed not hym that was crucyfyed / and adoured the sonne /. And thenne Heracle / whiche was armed wythe faythe / brought his hooste ageynst hym / and destroyed and wasted the Persyens with many batayles that he made to them / and made Cosdroe to flee unto the Cyte of thelysonte /. And atte the laste Cosdroe hadde the flyxe in his bely / And wolde therefore crowne his sone Kynge / which was named Mendasa /. And whenne Syroys his oldest sone herde thereof he made alyance with Heracle / And pursewed his fader with his noble peple / and set hym in

| 1 | The Legendary |

bondes / And fusteyned him with breede of trybulacion / and with water of anguysshe / And atte last he made to shote arowes at him bycause he wold not bileve in god & so deyde / & after this thynge he sente to Heracle the patriarke the tree of the Crosse and all the prysoners / And Heracle bare into Iherusalem the precious tree of the Crosse /. And thus it is redde in many Cronycles also /. Sybyle sayth thus of the tre of the Crosse / that the blessyd tree of the Crosse was thre tymes with the paynyms / as it is sayd in thystorie trypertyte O thryse blessyd tree on whiche god was stratched / This peradventure is sayd for the lyf of Nature / of grace / and of glorye / which cam of the crosse /. At Constantynople a Iewe entyred in to the chirche of seynt sophye / and consydered that he was there allone / and sawe an ymage of Ihesu cryste / and tooke his swerde and smote thymage in the throte / and anone the bloode guysshed oute /

and sprange in the face and on the hide
of the Iewe / And he thenne was aferd
and took thymage / and cast it into a
pytte / and anone fledde awey /. And it
happed that a Crysten man mett hym /
and sawe hym al blody / and sayd to
hym / fro whens comest thou / thou
hast slayne soume man / And he sayd I
have not / the crysten man sayd Veryly
thou has commysed somme homycyde /
for thou art all besprongen[1] with the
blood. And the Jewe said / Veryly the
god of Crysten men is grete and the
faythe of hym is ferme and approved in
all thynges / I have smyten no man /
but I have smyten thymage of Ihesu
Cryste / and anone yssued blood of his
throte /. And thenne the Jewe brought
the Crysten man to the pytte / and then
they drewe oute that hooly ymage /.
And yet is sene on this daye the wounde
in the throte of thymage / And the Iewe
anone bycam a good Crysten man, &
was baptysed / In Syre in the cyte of

[1] *Besprinkled.*

baruth there was a criften man / which had hyred an hous for a yere / & he had fet thymage of the crucifixe by his bedde to whiche he made dayly his prayers and faid his devocions / & at the yeres ende he remeved and tooke another hous / & forgate & lefte thymage behynde hym / and it happed that a Iewe hyred that fame hows / & on a daye he had another Iewe one of his neyghbours to dyne / & as they were at mete it happed hym that was boden[1] in lookyng on the walle to efpye this ymage whiche was fyxed to the walle and beganne to grenne at it for defpyte / and ageynft hym that bad hym / & alfo thretned & menaced hym bycaufe he durft kepe in his hous thymage of Ihefu of nazareth / & that other Iewe fware as moche as he myght / that he had never fene it / ne knewe not that it was there / & thenne the Iewe fayned as he had been peafyd[2] / & after went ftrayt to the prynce of the Iewes / & accufed that Iewe of that

[1] *Invited.*

[2] *Pacified, appeafed.*

History of the Cross.

whiche he hadde fene in his hous /
thenne the Iewes aſſembleden & cam to
the hous of hym / & ſawe thymage of
Iheſu Cryſt / and they took that Iewe
and bete hym / & did to hym many
iniuryes / & caſte hym out half dede of
their ſynagoge / & anone they defowled
thymage with their feet / & renewed in
it all the tormentes of the paſſion of oure
lorde / & and when they perced his ſyde
with the ſpere / blood and water yſſued
haboundauntly / in ſo moche that they
fylled a veſſel / whiche they ſet ther-
under / And thenne the Iewes were
abaſſhhed & bare this blood in to theyr
ſynagoge & and alle the ſeke men and
malades that were enoynted therwyth /
were anone guaryſſhed & made hool /
& thenne the Iewes told & recounted al
this thynge by ordre to the biſhop of
the countre / & alle they with one wyll
receyved baptyſm in the faythe of Iheſu
Cryſt / & the biſſhop putt the blood in
ampulles[1] of Cryſtalle & of glas for to

[1] *Ampullæ*, bottles or flaſks.

be kepte / & thenne he called / the Cryſten man that had lefte it in the hows / & enquyred of hym / who had made ſo fayr an ymage / & he ſaid that Nychodemus had made it / And when he deyde / he lefte it to gamalyel / And Gamalyel to Zachee and Zachee to Iaques / and Iaques to Symon / and hadde ben thus in Ieruſalem unto the deſtruction of the Cyte / and fro thennes hit was borne in to the Royamme of Agryppe of Cryſten men / and fro thennes hit was brought ageyne into my countreye / & it was left to me by my parentes by rightful herytage / & this was done in yᵉ yere of our lord ſeven honderd and fifty / and thenne alle the Iewes halowed¹ their ſynagogues in to chirches and therof cometh the cuſtoume that Chirches ben hallowed / For tofore that tyme the aultres were but halowed only / and for this myracle the chirche hath ordeyned / that the fyfte Kalendar of december / or as it is redde in another

¹ *Conſecrated.*

History of the Cross.

place / the fyfthe ydus of Novembre fhold be the memorye of the paffyon of oure lord / wherfor at Rome the chirche is halowed in thonoure of our favyour whereas is kepte an ampulla with the fame blood / And there a folempne fefte is kepte and done / and there is proved the ryght grete vertue of the croffe unto the paynyms and to the myfbylevyd men in alle thynges /.

And faynt Gregory recordeth in the thirdde booke of his dyalogues / that whanne andrewe Biffhop of the Cyte of Fundane fuffred an holy noune to dwelle with him / the fende[1] thenemy beganne temprynte in his herte the beaulte of her / in fuch wife / that he thought in hys bedde wycked and curfyd thynges / and on a daye a Iewe cam to Rome / and whanne he fawe / that the day fayled / and myghte fynde no lodgynge / he wente that nyght / and abode in the Temple of appolyn /. And bycaufe he doubted of the facrylege of the place /

[1] *Fiend.*

	how be hit / that he hadde no faythe in the Croſſe / yet he markyd and garnyſſhed hym wyth the ſigne of the Croſſe / then at mydnyght whan he awoke / he ſawe a companye of evylle ſprytes / whiche went to fore one / like as he hadde ſomme auctoryte puyſſance[1] above thother by ſubiection / and thenne he ſawe hym ſytte in the myddes among the others / and beganne to enquyre the cauſes and dedes of everyche[2] of theſe evylle ſprytes / whyche obeyed hym / and he wold knowe / what evylle everyche had doo / But Gregory paſſyth the maner of this vyſyon / bycauſe of ſhortnes / But we fynde ſemblable in the lyf of faders / That as a man entryd in a Temple of thydolles / he ſawe the devylle ſyttynge / and all his meyny[3] aboute hym. And one of theſe wycked / ſprytes cam / and adouryd hym / and he demaunded of hym / Fro whens comeſt thow / and he ſayd / I have ben in ſuch a provynce / and have moeved grete

[1] Power.

[2] Each or every one.

[3] Attendants.

History of the Crofs.

warres / and made many trybulacions and have ſhedde moche blood / and am come to telle it to the / and Sathan ſayd to hym / in what tyme hath thow done this / and he ſayd in thyrtty dayes and Sathan ſayd / why haſt thow be ſoo longe there aboutes / and ſayd to them that ſtode by hym / goo ye and bete hym / and all to laſſhe hym / Thenne cam the ſecond and worſſhiped hym / & ſayde Syre I have ben in the ſee / and have moeved grete wyndes and tormentes / & drowned many ſhippes / & ſlayn many men / and Sathan ſayde how longe haſt thow ben aboute thys / & he ſayd xxii dayes / & Sathan ſayd haſt thou done no more in this tyme / & commanded that he ſhold be beten / and the third cam / & ſaid / I have ben in a Cyte & have mevyd ſtryves and debate in a weddynge / and have ſhed moche blood / & have ſlayne the hoſbond / & am come to telle the / & ſathan ſayd / in what time haſt thou done this / & he ſaid in ten dayes /

& he fayd haft thou done no more in that time / & commanded them that were aboute hym to bete hym alfo / Thenne cam the fourth & fayd / I have ben in the wyldernefs fourty yere / and have laboured aboute a monke / & unnethe at the lafte I have throwen & made hym falle in the fynne of the flefshe / & when fatan herd that / he aroos fro his fete / & kyffed hym / & tooke hys crowne of his hede / & fet it on his hede / & made hym to fytte with hym / & fayde / thou haft done a grete thynge / & haft laboured more / than all thother / and this may be the maner of the vyfyon / that faynt gregorye leveth / whan eche had fayd / one fterte up in the myddle of them alle / & feyd he hadde mevid Andrewe ageynfte the name / & had mevyd the fourth part of his flefhe agenft her in temptacion / & therto / y[t] yefterday he drough[1] fo moche his mynde on her / that in the hour of evenfonge he gaf to her in Iapping[2] a

---

[1] *Drew.*

[2] *Jeft.*

buſſe[1] / & ſeid pleynly yᵗ ſhe muſt here it that he wold ſynne with her / thenne the mayſter commanded hym that he ſhold perform yᵗ he had begonne / & for to make hym to ſynne he ſhold have a ſyngular Vyctory and reward among alle the other /. And thenne commaunded he that they ſhold goo loke who that was that laye in the Temple / And they wente / & loked / And anone they were ware / that he was marked with the ſigne of the croſſe / And they levynge aferd eſcaped / and ſayd / veryly this is an empty veſſel / alas / alas / he is marked /. And with[2] thus wys alle the company of the wykked ſprytes vanyſſhed awaye / And thenne the Iewe al amoevyd cam to the biſſhop / and told to hym all by ordere what was happend / And whan the biſſhoppe herd this / he wept ſtrongly / and made to voyde all the wymmen oute of his hows / And thenne he baptyſed the Iewe.

Seynt Gregory reherceth in his

[1] *Kiſs.*

[2] *In this wiſe.*

dyalogues that a nonne entryd into a gardyne / and fawe a letufe / and coveyted that / and forgate to make the figne of the Croffe / and bote¹ it glotonoufly / And anone fylle doune and was ravyfthed of a devylle / And ther cam to her faint Equycyon* / And the devylle beganne to crye and to faye / What have I doo / I fatte uppon a lettufe / and fhe cam / and bote me / and anone the devylle yffued oute by the commaundement of the holy man of god /. It is redde in thyftorye Scolaftyke / that the paynyms had peynted on a walle the armes of Serapis / And Theodofyen dide doo putt them oute / and made to be paynted in the fame place the figne of the Croffe / And when the paynims & prieftes of thydolles fawe that / anone they dyde them to be baptyfed / fayenge / that it was gyven them to underftonde of their olders /

Bit.

---

* St. Equitius was a hermit, and looked after the welfare of other hermits and monks. He took a fpecial intereft in a convent of young virgins; died about A.D. 540.

that thofe armes fhold endure tyll / that fuche a figne were made then / in whiche were lyf / And they have a lettre / of whiche they ufe / y^t they calle holy / & had a forme that they faid it expofed and fignyfyed lyf perdurable.

Thus endeth the exaltacion of the holy Croffe.

Having read thefe extracts from the Golden Legend, we fhall be able to underftand the accompanying illuftrations, which reprefent fome frefcos of the fifteenth century, which formerly adorned the walls of the / Chapel of the Gild of the Holy Crofs, at Stratford-upon-Avon; which ftands clofe by New Place, Shakefpeare's houfe. Thefe frefcos, alas! no longer exift, for, in 1804, the Chapel underwent confiderable repair, during which, under the whitewafh, were difcovered traces of paint, and thefe, being fcraped, a feries illuftrating the legend of the Crofs was found in the chancel, which was built in 1450. In other parts of the Chapel were found representations of the Ressurection, and the day of Judgment, St. George and the Dragon, and the death of St. Thomas a Becket, besides others.

Luckily, a gentleman from London, a Mr. Fisher, was then staying at Stratford-on-Avon, and he drew, and painted them—afterwards, in 1807, publishing them—and it is from his sketches that these illustrations are taken. The barbarians of Stratford hacked the plaster on which the Holy Cross series was painted to bits, and whitewashed all the other paintings. It is presumed they still exist, for, when the Chapel was thoroughly restored in 1835, traces of the other pictures were visible under the whitewash.

These pictures of the Invention, and Exaltation, of the Holy Cross are especially interesting, not only on account of their age and artistic merit, but from the fact that they are of English work,

History of the Cross.

and show the English idea of treating the subject. I have reproduced them all but two; one, the fight on the bridge over the Danube between Heraclius and the son of Chosroes, and the other representing Heraclius smiting off Chosroes' head.

lxiv

A

Plate **A** reprefents the vifit of the Queen of Sheba to Solomon. Her name was Balkis, and, in her legendary hiftory, it is reported that Solomon, having heard of her riches and power, fent her a peremptory meffage to fubmit herfelf to his rule. She, dreading war with fo potent a fovereign, fent an embaffy to try and find out whether Solomon was as wife as he was reprefented to be. With this object fhe dreffed five hundred boys as girls, and a like number of girls as boys, and, among other prefents, fent a pearl, a diamond cut through in zigzags, and a cryftal box; and fhe fhould be able to judge of his wifdom and power, if he could tell the boys from the girls, pierce the pearl, thread the diamond, and fill the goblet with water that came neither from the earth nor the fky.

Needlefs to fay, Solomon paffed through the ordeal triumphantly. He ordered filver bafins to be brought, fo that the ambassadors' suite might wash their hands after their long journey, and the boys were easily distinguished from the girls, for they dipped their hands only in the water, whilst the girls tucked up their sleeves and washed their arms as well as their hands. Then he opened the box containing the pearl, diamond, and goblet, and, taking out the pearl, he applied his magic stone, Samur, or Schamir, which a raven had brought him, and which had the power of cleaving anything, and lo! the pearl was pierced; then he examined the diamond, which was so pierced that no thread could be passed through it; so he took a worm, and having placed a piece of silk in its mouth, it wriggled through, and the diamond was threaded. The next task was to fill the goblet, which he gave to a negro slave, and bade him mount a wild horse and gallop it till it streamed with sweat, and then to fill the goblet with it, thus fulfilling the imposed conditions. He then gave back thefe prefents to the ambaffadors, who fpeedily returned to Queen Balkis. She at once faw that it would be ufelefs to oppofe the powerful will of Solomon, and immediately fet out on her journey to that monarch.

It is here that her connection with the holy Crofs comes in, for its wood, which Solomon had cut down in order to incorporate it into his Temple, and which had the inconvenient property of fitting in nowhere, being either too long or too fhort for any purpofe, was in confequence thrown afide, and ultimately was ufed as a foot-bridge acrofs a brook. Acrofs this plank the Queen had to pafs, but fhe, recognifing its holy virtue, refufed to walk acrofs it, preferring to wade the brook, which, having done, fhe expounded its value to Solomon, and prophefied that out of it fhould be made the Crofs on which Jefus fhould fuffer.

She afterwards became one of Solomon's wives, and bore him a fon, and then

lxviii

B

returned to her own land, and from this son are descended the kings of Abyssynia.

The legend on the label is, as far as is legible, REGINA SABA FAMA SALOMONIS (adduct) A VENIT (Iero)SOLUMA UBI LIGNUM IN . . . ABATICA . . . IT . . . GENIS . . . PERSOLVETUR.

Plate **B** is, virtually, two; one showing the angel appearing to Constantine when, early in the fourth century, he was advancing towards Rome against Maxentius; but the legend of the miraculous inscription which appeared in the sky, "IN HOC SIGNO VINCES," does not appear. The other, and larger portion, represents his victory over Maxentius, and he is represented as spearing and killing that monarch; but this is not historically correct, for, after his defeat, as Maxentius fled towards Rome, essaying to cross the Tiber over a rotten bridge, it gave way, and he was drowned. It is noticeable that the Christian flag bears the Tau Cross.

The Plates **C** *and* **D** *run into each other, although they portray different subjects,* **C** *being the departure of St. Helena for Jerusalem on her quest of the holy Cross. The label in this fresco is utterly illegible.*

Plate **D** shows Judas (called Julius in the label) Cyryacus (the Quyryache of the Golden Legend) being released, after having been forced, through imprisonment and starvation, into confessing where the holy Cross lay buried. In the upper part St. Helena is receiving the holy Cross, whilst labourers are uncovering the Tau Crosses of the two thieves.

The legend is mutilated, but enough remains to make its meaning clear: "Here Seynte helyne examy(neth) the I(ews for) y^E Holy cros.... Iulius cyryacus (saith that he knew w)here hete was."

The legend in Plate **E** *is nearly perfect, and accurately describes the painting,* "Hyt was proved evidently by myrakel which was y^E very cros that oure Savyour suffyred.... In resynge a made from deth to lyfe."

শনি ০০০০

Here all the Crosses are of the Tau type, and the scene is laid in a forest, where an old labourer, and a billman, and the deer nibbling the trees, give a rural aspect, instead of in the City of Jerusalem, as saith the Golden Legend.

Plate **F** evidently consists of two separate paintings—one, where St. Helena is reverently carrying the Cross into Jerusalem, whilst the angels in heaven are discoursing celestial music; and the other, its reception either in Jerusalem or Byzantium, whither St. Helena sent a portion as a present to her son. And this latter seems the more probable, if we imagine the King, who, with St. Helena, is adoring the Crucifix, to be the emperor Constantine, a fact which might have been settled had the label been legible.

The legend at the bottom is unfortunately mutilated, but that evidently relates to that portion of the Cross which remained at Jerusalem, because it speaks

lxxii

G   H

of Chosroes: "Here the hole cros was broughte solemly yn to the .... in yᴇ bysshops hands easily and (remaynyd) un to the tyme of (King Codsd)roe.

Plates **G** and **H** reprefent the ftory told in the Golden Legend, of Heraclius bearing the Crofs into Jerufalem, how the gate miraculoufly clofed, and an angel appeared in the heavens and reproved Heraclius for riding in ftate on the very fpot where Jefus had gone in all meeknefs, and lowlinefs, to His paffion. The legend is erafed in parts, the unmutilated portion reading, "As the nobul kynge Eraclyus com rydyng towarde yᴇ cytte of Ierusalem beryng yᴇ crosse so grete pryde .... where yᴇ ...."

Naturally, the poffeffion of a piece of the true Crofs would be efteemed as a moft precious property. No matter how fmall, it would be reverentially enclofed in cryftal and gold, and was more than a prefent fit for an emperor or king, and we cannot marvel that fmall pieces were diftributed all over Chriftendom. Poffibly fome of the relics fhown as pieces of the very Crofs might not have been what they were fuppofed to be, but it is hard to believe what John Calvin* wrote about it :—

"And fyrft of all let us begynne to fpeake of his croffe, whereupon he was hanged. I know that it is holden for a certaintie that it was founde of Heline the mother of Conftantine the Romaine Emperour. I knowe alfo what certaine Doctours have written touching the approbation hereof, for to certifie that the croffe which fhe found was without doute the felfe fame on the whiche Iefus Chrift was hanged. Touchynge all this I reporte me to the thynge it felfe, fo much is there that it was but a folifh curiofitie of her, or at the leaft a folifhe

---

* I quote from the tranflation by Steven Withers, 1561.

and unconsidered devotion. But yet put the case it had ben a worke worthy of prayse to her, for to have taken paynes to fynde the trewe crosse, and that our lord had then declared by myracle that it was his crosse which she found; Yet let us onely consider that which is of our time. Every one doeth holde that this crosse which Helene founde is yet at Ierusalem, and none doeth doute thereof. Although the Ecclesiasticall history against sayeth the same notablye. For it is ther recited that Helene toke one part thereof to send to the Emperour her sonne, who put the same at Constantinople upon a fyne pyller of Marble in the myddest of the market. Of the other part, it is sayde that she did locke the same in a copher of silver, and gave it to the Bishop of Ierusalem to kepe. So then eyther we shall augment the historie of a lie or els that which is holden at this daye of the true Crosse, is but a vayne and triflyng opinion.

"Let us confider on the other part howe many peeces there are thereof throug out the worlde. Yf I would onely recite that whiche I coulde fay there woulde be a regifter fufficient to fyl a whole boke. There is not fo little a town where there is not fome peece thereof, and that not onelye in cathedrall churches, but alfo in fome parifhes. Likewife ther is not fo wicked an abbey where there is not of it to be fhewed. And in fome places ther are good great fhydes:[1] as at the holye chappell of Paris, and at Poitiers & at Rome, where there is a great crucifix made thereof as men faye. To be fhort, yf a man woulde gather together all that hath bene founde of this croffe, there would be inough to fraighte a great fhip. The Gofpell teftifieth that the croffe myght be caried of one man. What audacitie then was this to fyll the earth with pieces of wod in fuche quantitie, that thre hundred men can not cary them," &c.

---

[1] Blocks—billets

Calvin was full of zeal, and could not stoop to particularise. Witness his assertion that the Cross would freight a ship, and yet that three hundred men could carry it. M. Rohault de Fleury has gone very minutely into this matter. Knowing, from microscopical examination, that several of the relics of the Cross were of pine, he accepts this wood as his basis, and, from its probable size, he deduces a weight of 100 kilogrammes, equal to about 240 English lbs.; and, taking the average density of pine, he estimates that this would give 178 millions of cubic millimetres. He then describes all the known pieces in Europe, Jerusalem, and Mount Athos, with their measurements, and he puts the outcome at 3,941,975 cubic millimetres; thus, according to his shewing, there is but a very small portion of the Holy Cross in existence. I subjoin his list of the places in which pieces of the Cross are known to exist, as it is most interesting,

The Legendary

showing the comparative bulk of the pieces, in cubic millimetres:—

Aix la Chapelle	150
Amiens	4,500
Angers	2,640
Angleterre	30,516
Arles	8,000
Arras	10,314
Athos (le Mont)	878,360
Autun	50
Avignon	220
Baugé	104,000
Bernay	375
Besançon	1,000
Bologne	15,000
Bonifacio	47,960
Bordeaux	3,420
Bourbon l'Archambault	29,275
Bourges	22,275
Bruxelles	516,090
Chalmarques	,,
Carried forward	1,674,145

Brought forward	1,674,145
Châlons	200
Chamirey.	605
Chatillon	,,
Cheffes (Anjou) . . .	100
Chelles	,,
Compiègne	1,896
Conques	108
Cortone	3,000
Courtrai	200
Dijon	33,091
Donawert	12,000
Faghine	,,
Florence	37,640
Fumes	5,250
Gand	436,450
Gênes	26,458
Gramont	5,000
Jancourt (Aube) . . .	3,500
Jerusalem	5,045
Langres	200
Laon	,,
Carried forward	2,244,888

The Legendary

Brought forward	2,244,888
Libourne	3,000
Lille	15,112
Limbourg	133,768
Longpont	1,136
Lorris	,,
Lyon	1,696
Mâcon	2,000
Maeſtricht	10,000
Marſeille	150
Milan	1,920
Montepulciano	500
Naples	10,000
Nevers	176
Nuremberg	,,
Padoue	64
Paris	237,731
Piſa	8,175
Poitiers	870
Pontigny	12,000
Raguſe	169,324
Riel les Eaux	671
Carried forward	2,853,181

History of the Crofs.

Brought forward	2,853,181
Rome	537,587
Royaumont	,,
Saint Dié	99
Saint Florent	400
Saint Quentin	5,000
Saint Sepolcro	200
Sens	69,545
Sienne	1,680
Tournai	2,000
Trèves	18,000
Troyes	201
Turin	6,500
Venice	445,582
Venloo	,,
Walcourt	2,000
Wambach	,,
TOTAL	3,941,975

According to this table we are credited in England with 30,516 cubic millimetres of the holy Crofs, and it is interefting to know where they are fituated. M.

Rohault de Fleury, writing in 1870, fays there were pieces at Ifleworth; St. Gregory, Downfide, near Bath; in the poffeffion of Lord Petre; at Bergholt Eaft, in Suffolk; at Plowden; at the convent of St. Mary, York; at Weft Grinftead; at St. George's, Southwark; and Slindon, Suffex.

Thefe pieces of the holy Crofs are not large, as the following table, in cubic millimetres, fhows:—

At Ifleworth	1,000
,, College of St. Gregory .	6,120
Lord Petre (two relics) .	8,287
At St. Mary, Bergholt Eaft	1,008
,, Plowden Hall, Salop .	262
,, St. Mary, York (two relics)	5,600
,, Weft Grinftead ,,	38
,, St. George's, Southwark (four relics)	63
,, St. Richard, Slindon .	8,100
TOTAL . . .	30,516

One relic at St. Mary's Convent, York, is very fine; it is ornamented with scroll-work of the tenth century, and bears three impressions of the seal of the Vicar Capitular of the diocese of Saint Omer, 1657 to 1662. It is a pectoral cross that is supposed to have belonged to the patriarch Arnulph, who was with Robert, Duke of Normandy.

The other is supposed to have been attached to the above, and to have belonged equally to Arnulph, patriarch of Jerusalem. This is kept in a silver reliquary, which also contains relics of SS. Ignatius Loyola and François Xavier.

We see by the Golden Legend, that St. Helena, after finding the Cross, feeling certain that the nails were not far off, prosecuted a further search for them, and they were discovered "shynyng as gold." As with the fashion of the Cross, whether it was *immissa* or *commissa*, there is, and was, a controversy with regard to the nails, whether three or four.

Bosius in his learned and exhaustive book, *Crux Triumphans et Gloriosa*,* gives several authorities for three nails only—foremost, Gregory Nazianzen; but he does not give the passage where it may be found; the quotation, however, is

Γυμνὸν τρισήλῳ κείμενον ξύλῳ λαβών,

"having taken from the three-nailed wood the dead (or hanging) body." Thus clearly showing the number of nails he considered right.

Bosius then goes on to quote Apollinaris Laodicenus, who, in his tragedy entitled *Christus patiens*, called the holy Cross by the same words, τρισήλον ξύλῳ, "three-nailed wood"; and he also quotes from the *Meditat. vitæ Christi* of Bonaventura, "*Illi tres clavi sustinent totius corporis pondus.*" Nonnus, the Greek poet, writing in the fifth century, also says that our Lord's feet overlapped each other, and were

---

* From this book I have taken the head and tail piece here given.—J. A.

fastened by only one large nail. So that there is a very fair amount of antiquity in favour of three nails.

Against this theory may be quoted the authority of St. Cyprian, St. Augustine, St. Gregory of Tours, Pope Innocent III., Rufinus, Theodoret, and others, who say four nails were used in the Crucifixion of our Saviour. The battle waged pictorially; but perhaps the earliest known representation of the Crucifixion, that found in the Cemetery of St. Julian, Pope, or of St. Valentine in Via Flaminia at Rome, ought to bear most weight. Our Saviour is represented as being clothed in a long sleeveless robe, which reaches to His ankles; the feet are separate, and are each nailed. It is said that Cimabue was the first to paint the feet overlapping, and one nail. His example, however, was much followed, and hence the controversy.

Of these nails, universal tradition says that St. Helena sent two to her son

Constantine, and, as the Golden Legend has it, "the emperour dyd do fette them in hys brydel and in hys helme when he wente to batayle." One can underſtand one of theſe ſacred nails being worn in the Emperour's helmet as a preſage of victory and as a ſafeguard againſt danger, but the utility of incorporating one of ſuch priceleſs relics in a horſe's bridle is not ſo eaſy to comprehend; but the fathers of the Church, St. Cyril of Alexandria, St. Ambroſe, Theodoret, and St. Gregory of Tours, recogniſe in it the fulfilment of the prophecy of Zecharius, chap. xiv. 20: "In that day ſhall be upon the bridles of the horſes, HOLINESS UNTO THE LORD."

This bridle, or rather bit, is now ſaid to be in exiſtence in France at Carpentras, department of Vaucluſe. How it got there is not clearly known, but probably it was taken at the time of the Cruſades —as leaden ſeals on which it is engraved exiſt, attached to parchments of the dates

History of the Cross.

1226 and 1250, and it was mentioned in an inventory of relics in the year 1322. I have reproduced it, as well as the

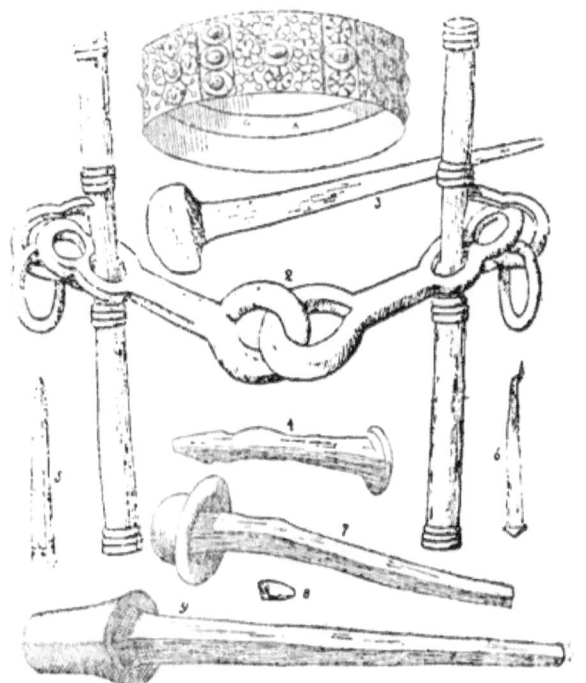

¹ The iron crown of Lombardy. ² The holy bridle at Carpentras. ³ Nail at Venice. ⁴ Nail at Rome in Sta. Maria in Campitelli. ⁵ Nail at Arras. ⁶ Nail at Colle. ⁷ Nail in the Church of the Holy Cross of Jerusalem, at Rome. ⁸ Portion of nail at Toul. ⁹ Nail at Tröves.

Iron Crown of Lombardy and the nails, from M. Rohault de Fleury's work, and, as will be ſeen, it is undoubtedly of great antiquity, cloſely reſembling the bits of the Romans.

According to Boſius, who quotes Gregory Nazianzen, a third nail was thrown by St. Helena into the Adriatic Sea, in order to calm a tempeſt; and the ſame authority ſays that the fourth was depoſited in the head of a ſtatue of Conſtantine, but this militates much againſt the number of holy nails ſaid to be in exiſtence. Calvin notices this, and is down upon it with ſledge-hammer force:—

"Yet there is a greater combat of the nayles. I wyll recite them only that are come to my knowledge. Thereupon there is not ſo lytle a childe but wyll judge that the Devyll hath to much deluded the worlde in takyng from it both underſtandyng and reaſon, that it coulde diſcerne nothynge in this matter. If the

History of the Cross.

auncient writers faye trewe, and namely Theodorite Hiftoriographer of the auncient churche, Helene caufed one to be nayled on her fonne's helmet, the other two fhe put in his horfe bitte. How be it Sainct Ambrofe fayeth not fully fo. For he fayeth that one was put in Conftantine's crowne, of the other his horfebit was made, and the thirde Helene kept. Wee fe y^t already more than twelve hundred yeres agone this hath bene in controverfie, to wit, what was become of the nayles. What certentie can be had of them then at this prefent time?

"Now at Millan they bofte that thei have y nayle that was put in Conftantine's horfe bitte. To the whiche the towne of Carpentras oppofeth herfelfe, fayinge that it is fhe that hath it. Nowe S. Ambrofe doth not faye that the nayle was knit to the bitte, but that the bitte was made thereof. Whiche thynge can in no wyfe be made to agre eyther w^t

their faying of Milan or wᵗ theirs of Carpentras.

"Moreover there is one in Rome at Sainct Helenes; another alfo at Sene, another at Venife. In Germany two: at Collyne one, at the three Maries: another at Triers, one in Fraunce at the holy chappell of Paris, another at yᵉ Carmes, one alfo at Sainct Denis in France: one at Burges: one at Tenaill, one at Draguine.

"Beholde here fourteene, whereof account is made; in every place they alledge good approbation for themfelves, as they fuppofe. And fo it is that everye one hath as good right as aunother. Wherefor there is no better way then to make them all paffe under one fidelium. That is to faye, to repute all that they faye hereof to be but lyes, feying that otherwife a man fhoulde never come to an ende."

What would Calvin have faid if he had feen the formidable lift of holy

nails enumerated by Guifto (or Juftus) Fontanini, Archbifhop of Ancyra? which is as follows :—
  1. Aix la Chapelle.
  2. Ancona, in the Cathedral.
  3. Bamberg.
  4. In Bavaria, Convent of Audechfen.
  5. Carpentras. The Holy Bit.
  6. Catania, Sicily.
  7. Colle, in Tufcany.
  8. Cologne.
  9. The Efcurial in Spain.
10. Milan.
11. Monza. The Iron Crown.
12. Naples. Monaftery of S. Patricius.
13. Nuremberg. Church of the Holy Virgin.
14. Paris.
15. Rome. Two Nails. Church of the Holy Crofs of Jerufalem; Church of Santa Maria in Campitelli.
16. Sienna. Hofpital Sainte Marie de de l'Echelle.

17. Spoleto.
18. Torcello, near Venice. Church of S. Anthony.
19. Torno, on the Lake of Como.
20. Toul.
21. Trèves.
22. Venice. Three nails.
23. Vienna.

But this lift is further fupplemented by M. Rohault de Fleury, who gives fix more :—

1. Arras, according to M. le Chev. de Linas.
2. Compiègne. A point.
3. Cracow, in Poland, according to M. Goffelin.
4. Florence.
5. Lagney.
6. Troyes.

So that no lefs than twenty-nine towns claim the poffeffion of thirty-two nails, all differing in form, the number of which can only be accounted for by the fup-pofition that only a portion of the holy nails has been incorporated into each of them.

One of the moſt intereſting relics in connection with the holy nails is the Iron Crown of Lombardy. This, as may be ſeen by reference to the illuſtration (Fig. 1), is a circlet of gold, ornamented with precious ſtones, and it is indebted for its name of "Iron" to a thin band (**A**) of that metal, which is inside the gold circlet. The Crown itſelf is of very antique form, being even devoid of rays, and is too ſmall to go on the head. Charlemagne was crowned with it in 774, and Napoleon did not think himſelf King of Italy until he had placed this precious diadem on his head, in 1805. It is kept at Monza, nine miles from Milan, in the Cathedral, which is of great antiquity. There it repoſes in a huge croſs placed over the altar.

Of the relics of the Croſs there now remains but two ſpecks of the title or inſcription thereon, and here, again, I am

xciv · The Legendary

The Title of the Cross.

indebted to M. Rohault de Fleury for the illuftration on page xciv., as it feems to me to be the beft yet publifhed.

The Evangelifts, although agreeing in the fpirit of the infcription, vary as to the letter.

Says St. Matthew: "This is Jefus the King of the Jews."
,, St. Mark: "The King of the Jews."
,, St. Luke: "This is the King of the Jews."
,, St. John: "Jefus of Nazareth the King of the Jews."

Neither St. Matthew nor St. Mark note the tri-lingual character, and SS. Luke and John vary as to the order of the different languages; the former faying it was in Greek, Latin, and Hebrew— the latter that it was in Hebrew, Greek, and Latin. The latter is the generally accepted form, and the reafon given is, that Hebrew, being the common language, it would naturally come firft, as we should do in an English notice, first in English, then, say in French and German, for the benefit of foreigners, as were the Greeks and Romans in Jerusalem.

The tradition is that, along with the Cross, St. Helena found the inscription, and that she sent it, together with a piece of the Holy Cross and a number of other sacred relics, to Rome, where it was deposited in the basilica of Santa Croce. Here it remained until Valentinian, fearing that it might fall into the hands of the Goths and Huns, hid it in the wall of the building, until it was found in 1492.

Valentinian died A.D. 375, and Antoninus Martyr, in his *De Locis Sanctis* (sec. 20), written about A.D. 570, says he saw the inscription which had been placed on the Cross, and that the words were, " Iesus Nazarenus Rex Iudæorum." He says that he held it in his hand, and kissed it, in the Church of Constantine at *Jerusalem*.

Hence it is evident that either tradition is incorrect, or that Antoninus did not tell the truth.

But the claim is that it is, and always has been, in Rome, and Bosius, in his *Crux Triumphans* (p. 60), gives an account of its re-discovery. He says that in February, 1492, Monseigneur Pedro Gonsalvo de Mendoza, Cardinal Sanctæ Crucis, was repairing and cleansing his church, and on the first day of that month, when the workmen reached the top of the arch which was in the middle of the basilica, and near the roof, they saw two small columns; and finding a space, they discovered a niche in which they found a leaden box, well closed, and on its lid was a tablet of marble, on which were engraved these words: HIC EST TITVLVS VERÆ CRUCIS. In this box was found a little board, about a hand's breadth and a half, much corroded on one side by time, and bearing, in grooved, engraved characters, which were coloured red, the following infcription: IESVS NAZARENVS REX IVDÆORVM. But the word IVDÆORVM was not entire, the laft two letters VM having crumbled to pieces by reafon of old age. The firft line was written in Latin characters, the fecond in Greek, and the third in Hebrew.

All the city went to fee it; and three days afterwards, Pope Innocent went alfo, and ordered the relic to be preferved in its box, and covered with a fheet of glafs. Every one was convinced that they had before their eyes the infcription which Pilate placed upon the Crofs over our Saviour's head, and which Saint Helena had depofited in the church at the time of its building.

The relic, as now feen, is very worm-eaten, but the letters are ftill vifible, and have been cut with a fmall gouge. They read from right to left, as Hebrew does, thus lending great plaufibility to the idea that it was done by fome Jewifh artificers; and it feems to be of fome

History of the Cross.

close-grained wood. Taking the piece now at Santa Croce, the whole inscription, if restored, would be thus:

The Inscription at Santa Croce, restored.

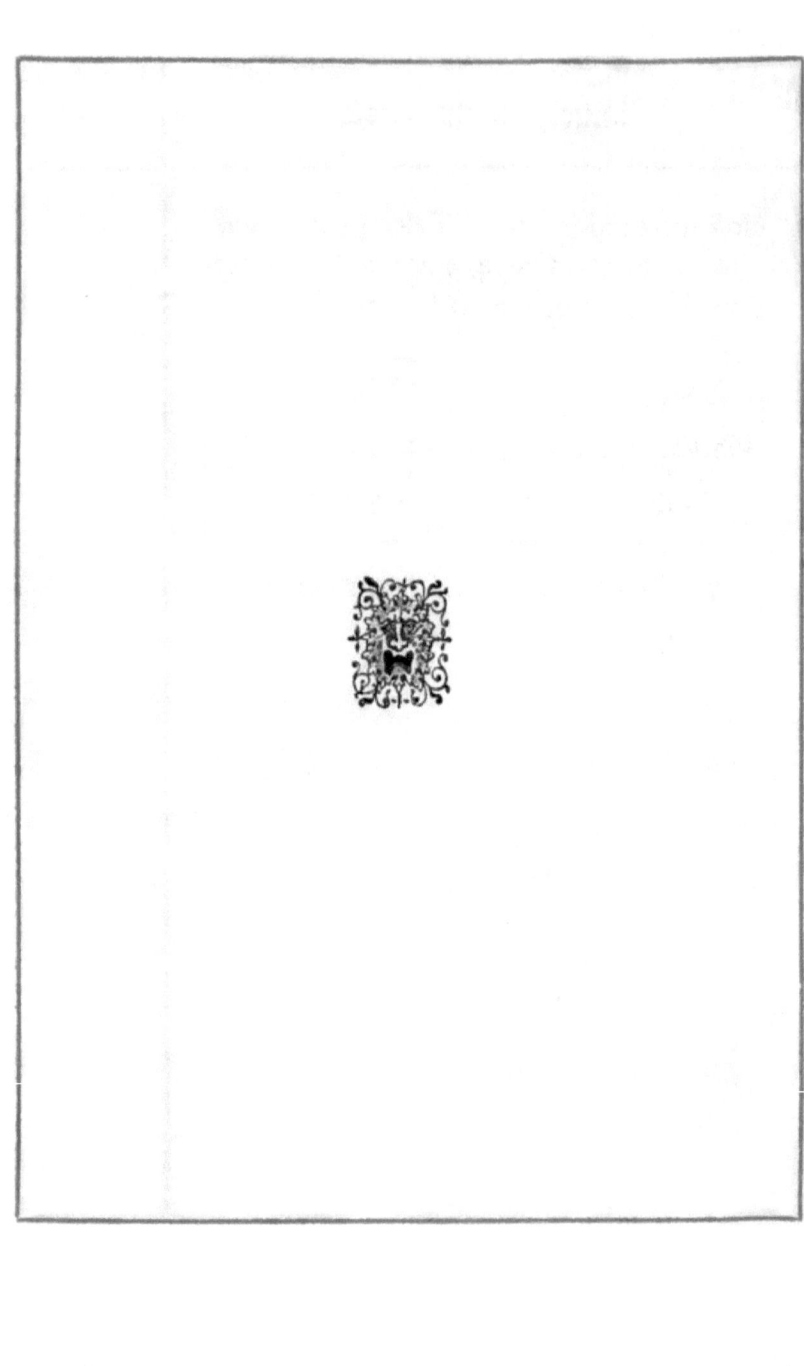

Notes on the Woodcuts.

HE History of the Legend of the Holy Cross which is here reproduced, is somewhat fuller than the Golden Legend of Caxton, there being particulars about Moses, David, and Solomon not to be found therein; but they may be found in other versions of the Legend, some in the Latin of Jacobus de Voragine, others in two MSS. in the British Museum.*

The engravings are taken from a very rare book, of which, as far as is known,

---

* Arundel, No. 507, and Add. MSS. 6524.

there are but three copies in exiſtence: one is in the Royal Library at Bruſſels, another at the Hague, in the collection of Mr. Schinkel, and the third is in the poſſeſſion of Lord Spencer at Althorp. It is from this book that theſe fac-ſimiles (made by M. J. Ph. Berjeau) were taken. The book itſelf has one woodcut on each page, with a verſe in Dutch, at the bottom, explanatory of each engraving. It is called indifferently *Hiſtoria Sanctæ Crucis* or *Boec van den houte* (Book of the wood or tree).

It was printed at Kuilenburg on March 6th, 1483, by John Veldener,* who had juſt removed from Louvain. Theſe ſixty-four engravings were originally on thirty-two blocks,† and evidently belonged to ſome much older block book, now

---

* His life and labours may be read in Mr. Hottrop's *Monuments Typographiques des Pays-bas—*.

† See *The Woodcutters of the Netherlands in the 15th Century*, by W. M. Conway, and an article by him in the *Bibliographer* of May, 1883, p. 32.

loſt. Theſe, Veldener cut in half, as he had already treated a *Speculum*, and brought them out as a freſh book.

The Legend as told by theſe engravings is as follows:—

Adam, feeling himſelf about to die, ſent Seth to Paradiſe to beg for ſome of the oil of mercy,[1] which, however, the Archangel Michael refuſed to give him, but, inſtead, preſented him with three ſeeds of the tree of life.[2] On his return, he found Adam dead, and, being unable to adminiſter theſe ſeeds to his father in any other manner, he put them under his tongue, and then buried him.[3] Preſently theſe ſeeds germinated and ſhot through the ground, and are traditionally ſaid to have been a cedar, a cypreſs, and a pine.[4] They grew until Moſes had led the Iſraelites out of Egypt, when he found them in the Valley of Hebron, and he recognized them as typifying the Trinity. He removed them, and they were his conſtant companions.[5] With them he

Woodcut No. 1.

No. 2.

No. 3.

No. 4.

No. 5.

smote the rock, and the waters gushed out,[6] and the bitter waters of Marah became sweet.[7,8]

He then planted them in the land of Moab,[9] and there they remained, until an angelic vision appeared unto David, and commanded him to go, and take them up, and bring them to Jerusalem.[10] On his return the three rods worked miracles, healing the sick,[11] and the leprous, with a touch;[12] nay, more, on being applied to three black men, they instantly became white.[13]

Arrived at Jerusalem, they wished to plant them, but for the night they left them in a cistern, by the Tower of David,[14] and lo! during the night, they struck root, and, entwining themselves, became but one stem,[15] which, when David saw, he had a wall built round it.[16] And the tree grew for thirty years, David ornamenting it with rings of sapphire and other precious stones, adding one for every year, and under this tree he com-

Woodcut No. 6.
Nos. 7, 8.

No. 9.

No. 10.

No. 11.
No. 12.

No. 13.

No. 14.

No. 15.
No. 16.

posed the Psalms, and praised God exceedingly.[17]

But Solomon, who must needs have all that was rare and costly to adorn his temple, cast his eyes upon this precious tree, and ordered it to be cut down.[18] It was duly felled, and squared, and trimmed, and it measured thirty cubits in length.[19] But when the carpenters came to put it into a place of that length, it was a cubit too short, and when it was fitted into a place of twenty-nine cubits, lo! it measured thirty, and the carpenters marvelled much, and were greatly astonished, and so, being useless, it was laid aside.[20] Yet the people came to see this wonderful tree, and amongst them was a maid named Maximilla, who sat down upon it, and instantly her clothes were in a blaze.[21] Then she began to lift up her voice, and prophesy, crying, "My God, and my Lord Jesu Christ."[22] Then the Jews took her, and scourged her to death.[23]

Woodcut No. 17.

No. 18.

No. 19.

No. 20.

No. 21.

No. 22.

No. 23.

	The Legendary
Woodcut No. 24.	The Jews, not knowing what to do with this miraculous tree, laid it acrofs a brook,[24] and, when the Queen of Sheba came to vifit Solomon, fhe recognized the virtue of the wood; and, refufing to defile it with her feet, fhe difmounted, and adored it, and waded through the brook.[25] Then, when fhe met Solomon, fhe reproved him, and told him that on that tree would the Saviour of the world fuffer death.[26] And Solomon commanded the holy wood to be taken up,[27] and caufed it to be carried into the Temple, there to be placed over the door, fo that all men might blefs, and adore it, and he coated it over with gold and filver.[28] There it remained until Abias ftripped it of its coftly coverings,[29] and the Jews buried it deep in the earth.[30]
No. 25.	
No. 26.	
No. 27.	
No. 28.	
No. 29.	
No. 30.	
	There it remained for many years, until the Jews wifhed to make a pool, where the priefts might wafh the beafts, to purify them, previous to facrificing them, and, unknowingly, they dug over

the burial-place of the Holy Cross.[31] This imparted such a virtue to the water of that pool, which was called Bethesda, that the sick were healed thereat, and an angel at times descended from heaven, and stirred the waters, and then whoever could get first into the waters was straightway healed of any infirmity he might have.[32]

We now come to the Crucifixion, and there was a lack of wood to make Christ's cross—when, suddenly, from the depths of Bethesda, leaped up the tree of the Cross, and floated gently to land. One ran to the High Priest,[33] and told him of the timely find of suitable wood, and he at once gave orders for it to be fashioned into a Cross.[34] Then comes the mournful procession to Calvary, with our Saviour fainting under the weight of the Cross, and Simon the Cyrenean is pressed into the service to help Jesus.[35] And then the Crucifixion.[36]

And whilst the crosses were still stand-

Woodcut No. 37.	ing, the disciples came to them and prayed, and many were healed of their infirmities, and many devils were cast out.[37] This so angered the Jews that they took the crosses down, and buried
No. 38.	them,[38] and there they remained until their invention by St. Helena, A.D. 326.
No. 39.	On her arrival at Jerusalem,[39] she convened a meeting of the principal Jews, and they denied all knowledge of it, but, on threat of being burnt, they said that one of their number, named Judas, knew
No. 40.	where the crosses were buried.[40] Judas, however, refused to tell, and, to compel him to impart his knowledge, St. Helena had him lowered into a dry well, "and there tormented hym by hongre and evyl
No. 41.	reste."[41] Seven days of this treatment made him submissive, and at the end of that time he capitulated. He was then
No. 42.	drawn up,[42] and prayed to God to direct
No. 43.	him to the right spot.[43] His prayer was heard, and after some digging, the crosses
No. 44.	were discovered.[44]

The news was brought to St. Helena, who visited the spot,[45] but although there were certainly three crosses, no one knew which was the one upon which Jesus suffered. A test, however, was applied, which proved to be satisfactory. The body of a maid was being borne on a bier for burial, but the funeral procession was stopped, and the body was touched by the different crosses. The two first produced no effect,[46] but when the third touched the dead maiden, she was at once restored to life.[47] Here, then, was proof positive; this was the very Cross; and St. Helena, mindful of her son Constantine, divided the sacred wood; part she enclosed in a case of precious metal, and kept at Jerusalem;[48] and part she sent to her son, at Byzantium, who received it with due reverence,[49] and deposited it in the church, with great ceremony.[50]

Here it remained, until it was taken away, with other spoil, by Chosroes, the

King of Perfia, who, aware of the sanctity of the relic, had it placed on the right hand of his throne. He was so puffed up with pride, that he ordered himself to be adored. His people, hitherto, had worshipped the sun, but now he ordained that henceforth he was to be considered the principal Person in the Trinity (the Father), and that the relic of the Cross was to be looked upon as the Son, whilst a golden cock which he had made was to represent the Holy Ghost.[51]

Woodcut No. 51.

Then Heraclius made war against Chosroes, and meeting with a Persian army under one of the sons of that monarch, it was agreed that, in order to prevent a useless effusion of blood, the two commanders should fight it out between them, and whoever was vanquished should submit.[52] The duel was fought on a bridge over the Danube, and Heraclius vanquished and killed the son of Chosroes.[53] The Persian army then made their submission,[54] and the penance

No. 52.

No. 53.
No. 54.

History of the Cross.

imposed upon them by the conqueror was that they should all be baptized, which was duly done.

Heraclius then went to Chosroes, and told him what he had done, offering him his life if he too would embrace Christianity,[55] but the Persian monarch refused, and Heraclius smote off his head.[56] He then crowned a son of Chosroes, and caused him to be baptized,[57] himself standing sponsor, and buried the slain king with befitting honours.[58] Then, taking possession of the holy relic,[59] he set out with it for Jerusalem. But, as he was bearing it in great state, he came to that gate of the City through which Jesus went to His passion, worn, buffeted, scorned, and weary, carrying the heavy burden of His cross. And suddenly the gateway became solid masonry, so that he could not pass through, and an angel appeared in the heavens, and reproved him for his ostentatious display in a place which his Saviour had previously trodden

Woodcut No. 55.
No. 56.
No. 57.
No. 58.
No. 59.

Woodcut No. 60.

No. 61.
No. 62.

No. 63.

No. 64.

in such deep humility.⁶⁰ Heraclius dismounted from his horse, and, stripping himself of all the trappings of royalty, barefoot, and in his shirt,⁶¹ he meekly bore the Cross to its appointed place,⁶² the masonry disappearing as soon as he had humbled himself.

A piece of the Cross was afterwards sent to Rome, where it duly arrived after a very stormy voyage,⁶³ and it was there preserved for the adoration of the faithful.⁶⁴

JOHN ASHTON.

Seth lieve sone wilt my wel verstaen
Totten pandise soe sult ghi gaen
Ende daer sult ghi den enghel vraghen
Wanneer dat eynden sullen mijn claghen

Adam sends Seth to Paradise for some of the Oil of Mercy.

cxiv 2

Hier gheeft hem die enghel drye greynen claer
Die sal hi begraven met sinen vader
Daer of sal wassen enen boeme goet
Daer Cristus aen sal storten sijn bloet

The Archangel Michael gives Seth three seeds of the Tree of Life.

Hier begravet Seth sinen vader
Ende hi nem die drie greynen claer
Ende hi heeft se onder sijn tonghe gheleyt
Als hem die enghel had te gheseyt

Seth buries Adam and puts the three seeds of the
Tree of Life under his tongue.

cxvi 4

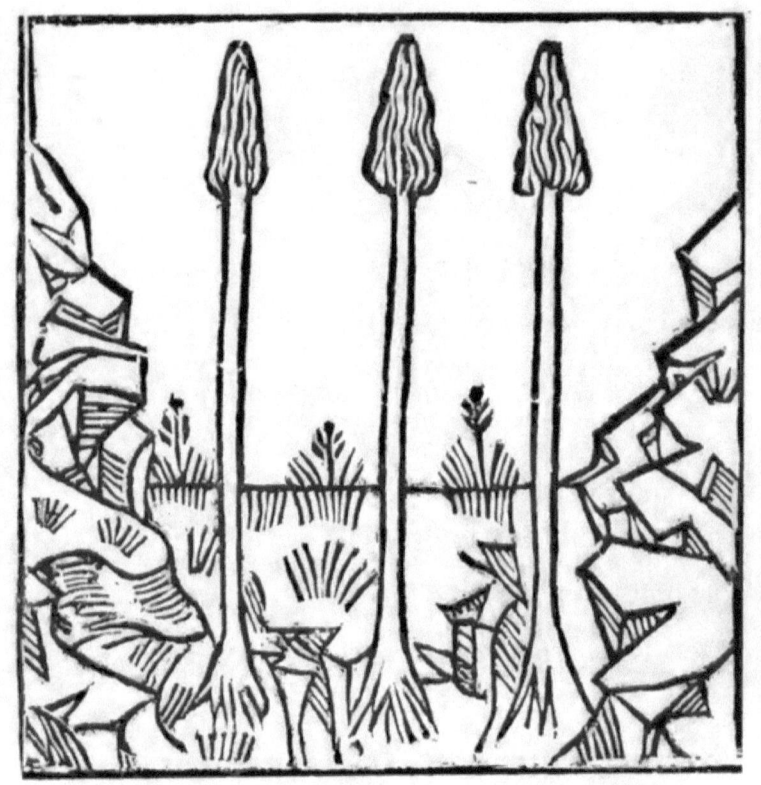

Hier sijn nv ghewassen drye roeden claer
Wt adams graf ende was seths vader
Ende die sijn daer bliuen staen
Tot dat se moyses van daer heeft ghedaen

The three seeds spring up.

5   cxvii

Hier rustet moyses in waren talen
Metten kinderen van ysrahel in enen dale
Daer soe siet hi staen al openbaer
Beneuen hem die roeden claer

Moses always has the three rods with him.

cxviii 6

Hier hebben si den berch gevonden
Ende si murmureerden ten seluen stonden
Ende si seyden daer al openbaer
Als dat dat water seer bitter waer

With them he makes water flow from the Rock.

Hier wet den enghel moyses verstaen
Dat hi die roeden soude slaen
In dat water dat zeer bitter was
Dat is ghewoiden soe als iclas

An Angel tells Moses how to sweeten the bitter waters.

Hier heeft moyses alsonder saghen
Die roeden int water gheslaghen
Ende si wechse daer weer
Ende dancte god onsen heer

Moses, by dipping the rods in the waters of Marah,
sweetens them.

Hier heft moyses die roeden gheplant
An dat eynde van moab nae onsen verstant
Daer soe sijn stoltuen staen
Tot datse dauid van daer heeft ghetuen

Moses plants the rods in the land of Moab.

An Angel appears to David and tells him to bring the rods to Jerusalem.

11 cxxiii

Hier reet dauid die roeden hoot
Vter derden ws sijt wel vroet.
Ende hi heeft er die steden mede ghesmeert
Ende si sijn van allen sieckten ghesont ghemaect

The rods heal the sick.

cxxiv   12

Hier weent dauid nae mijn verstaen
Een groot heer teekens ghepleecht
Die was metter lazarien beuaen
Thiwert ghesont wet oue die saelste verstaen

The rods heal a leper.

Hier coemt david metten roeden stoel
Ende sem comen drye swarte mannen te voren
Si wertese met die roeden saen
Ende doen soe worden si wit ghedaen

The rods turn three black men white.

Hier keuese dauid seer haestelijck
Tot iherusalem die roeden oetmoelijck
Ser soe moet hdi claerliken weten
Dat hese in sijn ... hooft gheslekten

David leaves the rods for the night.

15 cxxvii

Hier sijn die roeden binnen eenre nacht
Ghemet die goods hulpe ende cracht
Des wilt doch claerlijken nemen goem
Ende is gheworden eien sconen boem

In the morning he finds the rods have taken root and have become one tree.

cxxviii 16

Hier wert bauld tor selver dien
Sijn stofvaste ende wel bemueren
Oeck suldi dat claerlken verstaen
Wat si hierbij heeft doft ghedaen

David builds a wall round the miraculous tree.

David composes the Psalms and praises God, under the shadow of the tree.

Solomon orders the tree to be cut down and used in the Temple.

19   CXXXI

Hier gaen smeten ende mersten
Om den boem te seggen inden wercken
Si hebben ghemeten ende ghepast
Om inden tempel te leggen vast

Artificers fashion the tree.

cxxxii 20

Hier brenghen si dit hout te werck
Ende set is te wort riae sonn merck
Of hevis ghewoden alte lanck
Het bleef ouguwaert tesons soren tanck

The holy wood will fit nowhere.

Hier leyt dat hout in den tempel
Ende daer sce quam een vrouken simpel
Ende sis op dat hout ghesēten daer
Si verbrande haer clederen dat is waer

St. Maximilla sitting on the wood, her clothes catch alight.

CXXXiV 22

Hier coemt een prophetisse als ic verstae
Ende si was gheheten sibilla
Si prophetteerde al openbaer
Dat cristus soude hanghen in dat houte eraer

St. Maximilla prophesies concerning the wood.

Hier omme soe moeth bi voerwaer weten
Als dat die ioden sibilla hebben ghesmeten
Ende si hebben haer sulcken noot ghedaen
Dat si daer van die doot heeft ontfaen

St. Maximilla scourged to death.

CXXXVI   24

Hier hebben die ioden sulot verstaen
Dit hout ouer een ryuier ghedaen
Claerlijcken soe seldist verstaen
Om datmen duer ouer soude gaen

The wood used as a foot-bridge over a brook.

Hier nemt als wy verstaen
Die coninginne van saba ghegaen
Ende si maecte haer barvoet
Beneven den houte dat s'overvoet

The Queen of Sheba prefers wading through the brook, to walking over the holy wood.

CXXXVIII 26

Hier coemt vrou saba die coninghinne claer
En de si te spreke salomon al open waer
Wye dat hem maecte alsoe stout
Dat hi over een riviere leyde dat hout

The Queen of Sheba tells Solomon of the holy nature
of the wood.

Hier wet salom on die coninck
Slaen menighen schonen rinck
Van silver ende van goude claer
Ende dat hout daer xpristus in wilden openbaer

The holy wood is taken up.

The holy wood is carried into the Temple.

Hier coemt die derde coninck als ic las
Nae salomon gheheten abyas
Ende hi dede vanden houte nemen daer
Gout ende silver dat is waer

Abias despoils the holy wood of its precious covering.

cxlii 30

Hier comen die Joden ghegaen
Ende si hebben dat hout vten tempel ghedaen
Ende si hebben dat hout van deser weerden
Begrauen al onder die aerde

The Jews bury the holy wood.

Hier soe hebben knaepen daghen
Een piscine laten grouwen
Daer men in soude wasschen wilt verstaen
Die offerhande wert ghesloten

Digging the Pool of Bethesda.

cxliv 32

Hier coemt die enghel alle daghen
Tot tatter piscinen die is gheheiten
Wie dat naden enghel eerst tu water quam
Van allen sieten dat hi loes werdan

The sick being healed at the Pool of Bethesda.

33 cxlv

Doe ypristus stont in pylatus huys
Sy gheselten de seer confuys
Doen is bat hout van groten loven
Gheromen totter pistinen boven

The High Priest told of the discovery of the holy wood.

cxlvi   34

Hier hebben si ten seluen stonden
Dit hout in dat water gheuonden
Ende daer maecten si of een cruys
Dat ypristus droech seer consuys

The holy wood is made into the Cross.

Hier is ypristus metten cruys gheladen
Woer ons alre misdaden
Daeraen soude hi betalen gaen
Die sculd die adam hadde ghedaen

Christ bearing the Cross.

cxlviii 36

Hier hanghet cpriſtus aen den cruys
Ghelaſtet ende ſeer oonſuys
Ende heeft daer voldaen
Die ſcult die adam hadde ghedaen

The Crucifixion.

Daer stont dat heylighe cruys
Hier ghescheyde den duuel groot confuys
Want alle die gene die beseten syn
Die worden verlost van haerre pyn

Disciples adore the Cross, the sick are healed, and devils cast out.

cl 38

Hier omme soe waren die priesters quaet
Ende si namen aen hoorselven enen raet
Dat si dat cruys van groter weerden
Hebben gegraven onder die aerde

The Jews bury the Crosses.

Hier quam van romen helena
Si was keyserinne alsic verstae
Om te weten die waerheyt
Waer dit cruys is gheleyt

St. Helena comes to Jerusalem.

Hier coemt Helena ten seluen daghen
Ende si begij sint om dit cruys te vraghen
Ende si ontboet die Ioden alle gaer
Om te weten die waerheyt claer

St. Helena calls together the Chief Jews.

Hier heeft Helena Iudas
In enen put ghestellen als ic lus
Want si van hem woude weten daer
Waer dat dutwerde curps ghelegt waer

Judas is put into a dry well.

Ten eynde van seven daghen
Bestont Judas Helena te vraghen
Of si hem woude uten putte doen
Hi soude haer wysen dat cruys scoon

Judas is liberated from confinement.

Doe iudas quam tot deser stede
Soe dede hi oetmoedelic sijn ghebede
Doe seyde hem die enghel opēbaer
Dat daer tot crups ons heren waer

Judas prays for Divine direction.

Hier arbeydet Iudas al open baer
Om tevinden dat cruceclaer
Dat hi vant als die scrift belijt
Gervant si die nagbelen ter selver tijt

The Crosses are discovered.

Hier coemt oictus metten cruce gheten
Dat hi vonden heft wilt verstaen
Des brenct hi drye nagheten goet
Ende highoffe der keyserinnen ist tes vrat

St. Helena views the Crosses.

clviii 46

Nv en weten sinet al openbaer
Welc dat tcruys ons heren waer
So namen si die twee crucen daer
Ende sijt deen se op enen doden dat is waer

Trial of the true Cross.

47 clix

Doe sde namen si ter seluer stont
Dat derde cruys ende hi werd ghesont
Aldus wisten si die waerheyt claer
Als dat di cruys ons heren waer

A dead maiden raised to life by being touched by the true Cross.

St. Helena deposits a portion of the Cross in Jerusalem.

Hier brenct si des hilt leker ende vroet
Dat ander de stuc van den cruce goet
Constantino den Keyser openbaer
Si danckt god van den hemel dat is waer

St. Helena gives a portion of the Cross to Constantine.

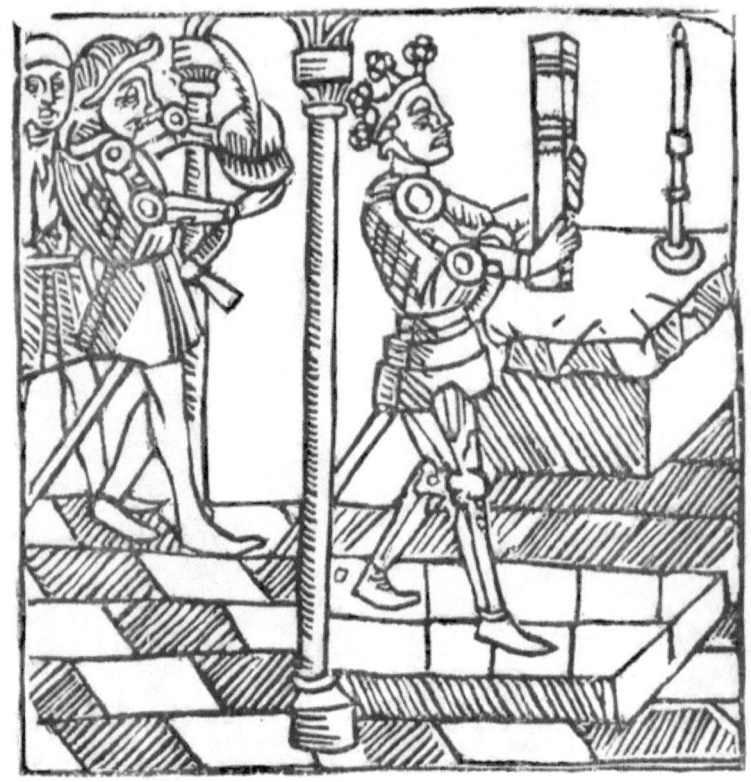

Constantine deposits his portion of the Cross in Byzantium.

51 clxiii

Hier sit cosdrus al openbaer
In sinen throen ende sept hi is duerbaer
Der hæet hi dat cruys die soen alsmen lest
Ende die steen hæet hi d ie heylighe gheest.

Chosroes commands his people to adore him.

Hier quam nu al openbaer
Een die eruelius seet dat is waer
Ende hi heeft enen strijt ghedaen
Teghens den longsten cosdroe wilt my verstaen

Meeting of Heraclius and Chosroes' son.

Desen strijt die is ghesciet
Op een brugghe die danubye hiet
Daer god eraclius den seghe gaf
Als dat hi den iongsten cosroe verwan

Heraclius fights the son of Chosroes and kills him.

clxvi 54

Hier coemt dat v ole wilt verstaen
En de si sijn tot eraclium alle ghegaen
En de si sijn ghecomen iont en de out
Elee samen in eraclius ghew out

The Persian army submit to Heraclius.

55 clXvii

Hier coemt eracliuß die keyser goet
Totten gnden woldras dat sijt vroet
Ende hi heeft hem tevoren gheseyt
Of hi woude aennemen die kerstenheyt

Heraclius visits Chosroes.

Hier heeft eracilius des ghploeft
Den tyranne of gheslaghen dat heeft
Hi ont sine sijn hen dat verslaet
Nae sijn eyghen sonden ende misdaet

Heraclius kills Chosroes.

57 c!xix

Hier is als wy moghen verstaen
Den ionghen coso de kersten ghedaen
Ende alle sijn volc des seluer sijt
Wert kersten ter seluer tijt

Heraclius crowns and baptizes the son of Chosroes.

clxx 58

Hier eraclius den ouden cosdroe beghraeft
Den iongen hi weder omme leyt gheeft
Ende hi gheeft hem weder alle tzader
Dat rijck dat toe plach te hoeren sinen vader

Burial of Chosroes.

Hier gaet eraclius met haestichayt
Ende neemt dat hout der heylicheyt
Ende hi toech daermede sonder oetmoet
Tot iherusalem als ick verstoet

Heraclius takes possession of the relic of the Cross.

Hier moechdi sien claerlijck
Dat die enghel sloet die poert seer rijcke
Ende seyt dat doer sijn oetmoet
Daer epuut in gincs bloetsvoets ende sonder oets

Heraclius, attempting to enter Jerusalem, is miraculously prevented, and is reproved by an angel.

Hier maect hem met haesten groot
Eraclius bloets hoeft en de baruoets
En de sijn ghecomen dat wel verstaet
Ootmoedelijc tot Iherusalem op die straet

Heraclius divests himself of state.

clxxiv 62

Hier coemt eraclius sekerlijck
Totten tempel seer oetmoedelijck
Eñ si brenct dat heylighe hout daert plach te staen
Oetmoedelijck heeft hi hem ghebuet ghedaen

Heraclius places the relic of the Cross in its appointed place.

Hier sijn die pluden in groter noot
Ende si meenden hier te bliuen doot
Si aenbeden dat heylighe cruys oetmoedelic
God die heeft se verlost sekerlic

A portion of the Cross is sent to Rome, the vessel bearing it meeting with a storm.

The relic of the Cross exposed for adoration.

www.ingramcontent.com/pod-product-compliance
Lightning Source LLC
Chambersburg PA
CBHW032153160426
43197CB00008B/895